P.E. BAYLEY MAY 2003

The nature of Barbel

by

Nick Giles

Foreword by Chris Yates

Perca Press

1

First published in 2002 by:

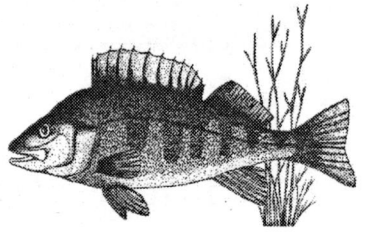

Perca Press, 50 Lake Road, Verwood, Dorset, BH31 6BX.

Tel 01202 824245 · Fax 01202 828056 · e-mail nickgiles@cix.co.uk

© Nick Giles, Perca Press 2002.

All rights reserved. No part of this publication may be reproduced or transmitted in any form or by any means, electronic or mechanical, including photocopy, recording or any information storage and retrieval system, without permission in writing from the publishers.

ISBN 0-9543239-0-4

Illustrations: © Nick Giles
 © Chris Yates, Clare Yates, Edward Barder, Peter Gathercole, Dave Burr, Ian Watson, Pete Reading, Colin Whitehouse and © MGN - a Trinity Mirror Business 2002.

Mr Crabtree Goes Fishing is available from Ronnie Butler on 020 7526 2328.

The Nature of Barbel was printed and bound in the UK by:
The Minster Press, 5 Mill Lane, Wimborne, Dorset, BH21 1JQ.
Tel. 01202 882277 · www.printsolutions.co.uk

Foreword

'The barbel', said Dick Walker, 'is a more mysterious fish than the carp'.

Almost fifty years ago, Walker was one of a little group of anglers who were exploring the barbel potential of the Hampshire Avon. At that time, all that was known about the river's barbus population was that the Royalty Fishery supported a large head of very big fish while the rest of the river contained a very small head of even bigger fish. Walker, who'd only recently emerged from a twenty-year addiction to carp fishing, had discovered the whereabouts of two colonies of absolute monsters along the Avon's middle reaches. Apart from a couple of river keepers and a few salmon anglers, no-one else knew anything about these fish; certainly no-one had ever deliberately fished for them. So Walker and his mates began a campaign of observation, groundbaiting and intensive angling. Several times they were able to cast their hook-baits to barbel that had to weigh at least twenty pounds, but they hardly ever drew any response. Mostly, the fish would simply disappear after a few hours, never to be seen again. Of the few fish that were actually hooked and landed, only two were over ten pounds, the largest being a 'mere' twelve pounder. So, after a few enthralling but ultimately frustrating seasons, the campaign ended and Walker went off to fish for trout.

I wonder what Walker would make of the situation now, at the beginning of the twenty first Century, when the Avon's barbel population has since exploded along the middle reaches and is now seemingly in decline whilst rivers like the Wye, Severn and Teme have become paradises for barbel anglers and the Great Ouse, Walkers home river - once just the home of barbel rumours, has produced a string of astonishing, and astonishingly unexpected monsters. Certainly, because of the much wider distribution of barbel, there are now many more barbel anglers than when Walker first fished for them. Also, barbel fishing has replaced carp fishing as the thinking angler's favourite occupation, generating more discussion and more writing about the subject than at any previous time.

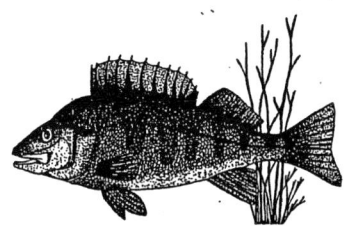

Perca Press, 50 Lake Road, Verwood, Dorset, BH31 6BX.

Tel 01202 824245 Fax 01202 828056 e-mail nickgiles@cix.co.UK

The nature of Barbel

Dear Customer

Thank you for your order for The nature of Barbel.

We hope that you enjoy reading it.

Best wishes

Nick Giles

Perca Press is an imprint of Nick Giles Associates, consultants: freshwater fisheries, conservation & wetland ecology.

But is the fish itself any less mysterious than it seemed before?

We are definitely more aware of the barbel's habits, of its dietary requirements, its preferred environment, its unique characteristics, yet, until now, nobody has actually been qualified or informed enough to join up all these scraps of knowledge and form a more complete picture of this remarkable fish. But Nick Giles, being a crazed barbel angler as well as a highly respected fisheries consultant and freshwater biologist, has done more than simply put together a jig-saw of already known facts. By also applying his own experience, his own observation and his own analysis, he has created a whole new picture.

The nature of barbel is a wonderfully original book, full of good sense, good ideas, good descriptions and good science. By raising the fish out of its rather shadowy depths, it allows us to more clearly appreciate and understand it. But even Nick would agree that, despite his years of study, the barbel will never be completely understood. While unlocking many long-pondered secrets, his book leaves the fish's essential mystery almost intact. And though, by reading it, we'll become more complete barbel anglers, we mustn't forget that the fish will always have the last swirl.

But now here's a mystery: how come I'm sitting at home scribbling on a perfect summer evening, when I know that Nick is somewhere along the Avon, fishing for barbel? Could it be that he promised to buy me a pint if I wrote him this today, or was it simply that he wanted a certain favourite barbel pool to himself?

Whatever the reason, I think this will do for the moment. Now, where's my rod.......

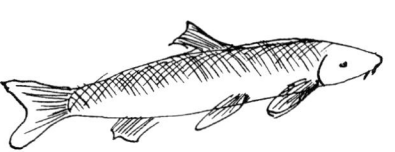

July 15th 2002.

Contents

Foreword	By Chris Yates	3
Thanks		9
Dedication		10
Chapter 1	Conservation and coarse fishing	11
Chapter 2	Understanding barbel ecology	19
Chapter 3	River habitats	59
Chapter 4	Fishery management on barbel rivers	87
Chapter 5	Ecological coarse fishing	107
Chapter 6	Recommended Reading	169

Thanks

Many thanks to all the following for their contributions, help and encouragement:

Chris Yates (Foreword, photos and for being an 'all-round good egg'). Clare Yates (superb drawings). Edward Barder, Charles Barder, Nick Bubb, Dave Burr, Chris Gardner, Peter Gathercole, Garry Lee, Dave Mattey, Tim Pryke, Pat O'Reilly, Pete Reading, Dave Wettner, Colin Whitehouse, and Ian Watson (articles, photos, scanning and good advice). Mirror Group Newspapers; MGN Ltd - a Trinity Mirror Business 2002 (copyright holders of Mr Crabtree cartoons and Ronnie Butler for his help with permission to use them). Nick Bubb for the gift of a large pile of Anglers Mails. Thanks also to Nick for the look on his face when both Ian Watson and I caught barbel larger than his personal best whilst fishing either side of him on the River Wye. Days spent on the riverbank with old friends are a good bit better than those spent in the office!

Dedication :

To the memory of Bernard Venables, 1907 - 2001.
The original Mr Crabtree.

© Bernard Venables

CHAPTER
1
Conservation and coarse fishing

This book is about coarse fishing rivers, how to better understand them and fish them for barbel. I have chosen the barbel because of its popularity, its importance in river fish communities and because I enjoy barbel fishing so much. I hope that both anglers and conservationists will find this book useful and a good read. Companion books, also to be published by Perca Press on lake fisheries for carp and tench, stream fisheries for trout and grayling and salmon and sea trout rivers are in preparation.

But first, the barbel………..

Sleek, handsome, immensely strong, guileful, stealthy - barbel can be a real challenge to locate, let alone catch and so remain interesting for many a long season. Izaak Walton (in The Compleat Angler, 1653) noted that:

> '*This fish is of a fine cast and handsome shape…….he loves to live in very swift streams or where it is gravelly or on Piles about Weirs or Floodgates or Bridges, that the water be not able, be it ever so swift, to force him from the place which he seems to contend for…..*

and
' is so strong that he will often break both rod and line'.

No wonder so many anglers can't wait to catch a barbel - and the popularity of the species is increasing. Anglers are natural conservationists - at the very least, they want to ensure good sport in future and so tend to look after their fisheries and fish stocks. Enthusiasts, and there are many, end up getting as interested in natural history as they are in catching fish. No angler is happy to see fish and other wildlife killed by pollution or habitats wrecked by over-abstraction, intensive agriculture or insensitive flood defence and land drainage schemes. Anglers are, therefore, often the people who campaign for better environmental quality of rivers and lakes.

Most freshwaters are fished - hundreds of thousands of freshwater anglers make for a very effective network of pollution watchdogs on river and lake banks. Also, in well-organised clubs and syndicates, winter working parties try to manage waterside habitats in a wildlife-friendly way. Whilst some are overly keen on cutting back trees, reeds and removing deadwood, opportunities both for angling and for conservation are generally maintained and improved. Some clubs get involved in ambitious habitat improvement projects and these can make a huge difference to fisheries and conservation. The close season for coarse fish on rivers allows a wealth of wildlife to breed in peace.

Successful anglers are good observers of nature; they learn to 'read' rivers and to weigh up the rhythms of activity rippling through lakes. Maybe the origins of this deep interest lie in our hunting ancestry - then, catching food was a life and death set of skills. Now, in an increasingly affluent society, coarse anglers fish for recreation, rather than for sustenance. Not long ago - not much more than an angler's lifetime - things were quite different.

In J.L.Webb's account of his 1940s midnight battle with a mighty 12lb Thames barbel which he fought for around three hours and finally landed, the barbel would have been lucky to survive. Webb would have killed it to sell as food - he was, after all, a Thames Registered Fisherman, presumably eking a modest living from the river in an age when coarse fish of all species were routinely eaten. There is nothing wrong with taking a sustainable crop from a natural resource but modern pressures on wild fish stocks mean that catch-and-release is now essential on most natural waters.

The link between stewarding fish stocks for food and avoiding overexploitation has a long history. Way back in the 1500s, during the reign of Queen Elizabeth I, a statute was passed by Parliament whereby anyone taking barbel of less than twelve inches should:

'pay 20 shillings, give up the fish so wrongfully taken and forfeit the net or engine so unlawfully used'.

Stiff penalties indeed - fish conservation started quite a while ago.

Coarse fishermen in Sheffield and London pushed via Mr Mundella for The Freshwater Fisheries Act of 1878 which enshrined the current coarse fish close season - March 15th - to June 15th. The first offenders were convicted at Newark on April 14th 1879 and fined 5 shillings - a lot of money in those days. The close season for coarse fish on rivers remains to this day but is under attack from those elements of the sport who argue that spawning fish are seldom caught and are returned anyway if they are caught. Traditionalists argue that it is good for fish stocks, waterside wildlife and the reputation of angling as a responsible pastime to give fisheries an annual rest. I'm in the latter group but have to admit that many coarse rivers are disturbed by other river users through the spring, fished by game anglers during the coarse fish close season and many coarse fish spawn after June 16th anyway. Time will tell whether the river close season is here to stay.

When the close season came into being, fish really needed a measure of protection - traditional barbel recipes included baking, stuffing with boiled eggs and mushrooms, poaching in white wine with onions and mushrooms or frying in butter with lemon juice and seasoning. Early writers were not, however, keen on the prospect of barbel roes for supper;

'The barbell is soft and moist, of easy concoction, and very pleasant taste; of good nourishment, but somewhat muddy and excremental. ....The spawn of them is to be objected to as most offensive to the belly and stomach'.

(T.Venner in Via Recta ad Vitam published in 1650).

'Beware of barbel : their spawn is surfeiting and dangerous, and whoever eats thereof, will break out in blotches, and red spots, will loath his meat, lose his appetite, and be extremely disorder'd. His liver is likewise unwholesome'.

(G.Smith in The Gentleman Angler published 1726).

In 1948, when the peerless Bernard Venables wrote the seminal 'Mr Crabtree goes fishing' it was regarded as routine for specimen coarse fish to be killed and sent to the taxidermist. The origins of size limits and of the closed season for coarse fish were based in the need to protect fish stocks from over-exploitation, especially when spawning. Nowadays, times have changed and a UK-captured barbel won't be on the menu - it may only have to suffer the indignity of being weighed and photographed before being returned carefully to the water. Better still, the fish is slipped from a barbless hook while still in the water - this is, by far, the least damaging method of releasing any fish. Be careful to check that barbel have recovered sufficiently from the fight to swim strongly away after release, otherwise just be patient and support the fish head-upstream until it's ready to go.

Conscientious coarse anglers do little harm to fish and do a lot to look after fisheries.

Some anglers contribute much of their free time to river and lake management - this is, of course, enlightened self-interest; excellent self-sustaining fisheries must be based on good habitat quality and good habitats need regular well-targeted management to keep them up to par. Creating complex cover, for instance, gives fish the chance to escape both intense predation pressure from cormorants or mink and too much pressure in over-fished swims. No fishery should allow anglers access to all the water - big patches of dense willow scrub, reeds or brambles will deter even the most determined jungle-bashers and create effective fish sanctuaries.

Where barbel stocks are little fished, fish remain relatively easy to catch, even during the day. When caught regularly, however, they learn quickly to avoid baits and situations which they associate with danger. I have watched shoals of barbel on the middle Wye edging sideways to allow trundled baits to pass by before returning to their preferred lies on the river bed. This probably happens all the time on many fisheries and perhaps with most fish species. Unless we fish at close range on shallow clear rivers we just don't often see what's happening at the 'business end' of the tackle.

Perhaps, on hard-fished waters, barbel and other cautious fish are only tempted to accept baits by especially good presentation, novel or natural offerings or by competition from close neighbours in the shoal. Regular ground-baiting, for instance with feeder-fed hemp, maggots, pellets or specialist pastes and boilies, may help to overcome these inhibitions. Also, fishing quiet, out of the way swims with a stealthy approach pays dividends. Barbel are generally well able to detect our often half-baked attempts at deceiving them but, over the course of a lifetime, a barbel may make a few mistakes and be caught many times.

Double figure barbel are, at least, teenagers and can be twenty, thirty or more years of age. Once the fish has reached its maximum length, it simply fluctuates in weight according to health, degree of sexual maturity and time of year. An example of a known thirty year-old barbel, caught from the Kennet by Edward Barder is described later in the book. These leviathans are very valuable to a fishery and, because it takes ages for barbel to grow to specimen size, it becomes vital to look after them. With care, a mature barbel can live a long life and spawn many times, helping to sustain the fishery and to provide anglers with occasional opportunities to catch and admire a monster. Barbel can be caught and released many times during their lives with seemingly little harm - good handling and the use of suitable gear are, however, important to get right. Padded unhooking mats help protect fish which are landed and barbless hooks cause little damage and are very easy to remove.

Luckily, barbel can be so canny that, even on heavily-fished rivers like the Hampshire Avon, Dorset Stour or Kennet, it seems likely that some fish, including many big ones, may only rarely be caught. Observations of barbel around baits show that, without any doubt, these fish (like their close cousin the common carp) can detect lines, hooks, odours, unusual movements of baits, colours, textures, vibrations, glimpses of anglers on the bank, etc, etc. Sometimes I wonder how we catch any barbel at all!

This formidable range of well-tuned senses is, of course, a real boost to barbel conservation and management - these fish are pretty good at looking after themselves. The best river coarse fisheries are, then, managed in a non-intensive way; fish need areas where they can avoid capture and the time and space to breed in peace. Recently, I was fortunate enough to catch a double figure Hampshire Avon barbel during a mild drizzly October dusk. Not my biggest barbel but probably the most majestic. The fish finally took the bait after long inspection, fought very hard and was scale and fin perfect - not a fish which had experienced too much fishing pressure and a pleasure to catch and return; it soaked me with a departing thrash of its tail.

My abiding memory of that two hour fishing session is not, however, the barbel, but the views of kingfishers, flocks of long-tailed tits, a greater-spotted woodpecker tracking insects in a rotten willow stump, a wheeling buzzard and then, at dusk, a barn owl floating over the darkening water meadows. Bliss.

I went home happy, appreciating that a fine fishery exists amid a rich wildlife community, in harmony. The substantial income from Christchurch Angling Club encourages Avon owners to ensure that the river and adjacent lakes are looked after - both for fish and for the other wildlife which shares their habitats. The estate and the club co-operate to improve the river - for instance at Ibsley where several kilometres of side streams and carriers have been cleaned out in recent years. Barbel have been stocked on some stretches to boost numbers of young fish - this may be crucial for long-term fishery performance although I would like to know why the natural spawning success of Avon barbel appears to be so poor. It may be a lack of shallow, sheltered gravel-bedded areas where young barbel can avoid the main force of the current or, perhaps, the chalk aquifer-fed Avon is too cool in most summers for barbel fry to survive in any numbers. Alternatively, perhaps, the silt that is known to choke salmon and trout redds in our local rivers is also affecting gravel-spawning coarse fish species. More research needed, I think.

Last summer I found a half-eaten eel further downstream on the Avon at Bisterne. The tooth marks on the fish and tracks in the mud told me that an otter frequents the wet willow scrub and reed beds which are allowed to flourish on this excellent fishery. The otters pose no threat to the quality of the fishing and the income from the fishing pays the keeper to manage the river in good heart both for fish and the otters.

Angling often provides an economic underpinning for the conservation of aquatic habitats which might otherwise be over-abstracted, polluted or ravaged by overly ambitious development. Anglers help to look after and pay to use fisheries - they have a stake in and appreciate the natural environment. By buying rod licences anglers help fund the Environment Agency to 'maintain, improve and develop' salmon and freshwater fisheries in England and Wales. The Agency does much valuable work, for instance on fisheries, conservation and the regulation of water quality, abstraction and other forms of industrial impact on rivers and wetlands . Where serious pollution occurs the Agency will often litigate. In other cases the Anglers Conservation Association (ACA) provides members with an excellent advice service through legal eagle Peter Carty and has a long track record of successful prosecutions of polluters.

At a time when some people wish to abolish angling on ethical grounds, fishing needs to fight its corner. Truly environmentally-friendly fishermen are most likely to carry public opinion with them and so continue to enjoy their pastime in the long-term. Some of our best known and most active conservationists are either anglers or, at least, appreciate the positive environmental role that angling can fulfil. The ranks of barbel anglers are swelling and our combined efforts can bring a brighter future for angling. The Barbel Society is a good example of a conservation-conscious angling organisation, striving to improve our river fisheries for barbel and all other fish too.

If we anglers and conservationists don't look after rivers and lakes for future generations, who will ?

© Clare Yates

CHAPTER
2
Understanding barbel ecology

© Clare Yates

Origins

About 12,000 years ago much of the British Isles was frozen in the grip of the last Ice Age. Whilst now we worry about global warming, Stone Age man was noticing things getting decidedly nippy. As glaciers pressed southwards, gouging out the valleys of our modern day Lake District and depositing the clays which carry many lowland river systems, freshwater fish were forced south into France. Land was frozen into permafrost and tundra zones; southern England and France were linked by a land bridge which, with rising sea levels, eroded away and sank under the Channel as the ice fields eventually retreated. As the last lowland ice thawed and warmer waters moved back northwards, fish from northern European river systems came with them, exploiting newly available pristine habitats throughout the British Isles. Imagine a world clad with birch, hazel, alder, willow and oak with crystal streams and no roads, towns, factories or pollution - wonderful. The damage which man has managed to wreak in the past 10,000 years (most of it in the last 200 years or so) is truly horrifying.

Cool, clean seas must have teemed with life as migratory fish joined those freshwater species which managed to recolonise the British Isles from the European mainland. Probably, only eastern England harboured natural stocks of coarse fish other than eels. Even today, warm-water fish species still predominate in the south of Britain while salmonids reign supreme in the north. Fish distribution is now a complex mix of natural colonisation overlain by the activities of generations of fish stockers. Some introductions have produced wonderful new fisheries and seem to have done little or no harm whilst others have devastated natural fish communities and threatened rare species. Think before you stock; once the fish are in there, it's often very difficult to get them back out.

Do you ever wonder where the current distribution of barbel in the British Isles came from? Alwynne Wheeler and David Jordan have researched this topic and the history is fascinating. It appears that barbel naturally colonised the Yorkshire Ouse, Derwent, Wharfe, Aire, Swale, Don, Trent, Witham, Welland, Great Ouse and Thames systems. Other, smaller, rivers such as the East Anglian Wensum, Yare and Stour may also have had pockets of fish. Barbel are, then, native to east coast English rivers. From these stocks barbel were deliberately moved around the country. This started at least as early as the 1890s, for instance, in 1896 when barbel (it is thought from the Thames) were stocked into the Dorset Stour - a beautiful river which proved very suitable for them. Barbel from the Rivers Lea and Kennet were stocked into the Hampshire Avon and some Stour fish may have migrated around the Clay Pool at the head of Christchurch Harbour to colonise the Royalty Fishery on the lower Avon. The Royalty may, however, have been separately stocked. Whatever their source, barbel have since colonised the Avon all the way upstream to Salisbury and beyond. Most anglers visiting the Avon below Salisbury probably now do so principally for the barbel fishing, rather than for salmon or trout.

In 1956 the Severn received a consignment of just over 500 Kennet barbel, these fish thrived and spread into key tributaries - the Vyrnwy, Tern, Worfe and Teme. In 1964 barbel from the Swale were released in the Warwick Avon, now a noted big fish water. The 1950s and 60s saw a series of stockings of Kennet barbel into the Bristol Avon which proved to be greatly to their liking. Subsequently, barbel have been moved into the Somerset Frome and the River Chew. In Northumbria the lower Wear and Tees acquired barbel mysteriously, adding to north country Yorkshire stocks, for instance, in the Rivers Swale, Wharfe, Aire, Calder and Don. In Wales, stocking (possibly from the nearby Severn) has produced barbel populations in the Wye, Usk and the Welsh Dee. Lancashire's Ribble was legally stocked with barbel relatively recently and they are also present in the Dane, Dove, Weaver and Bollin. Other stocks are present in the Kentish Stour and the Medway.

The last 50 years have seen a huge increase in readily available inexpensive barbel fishing - a great recreational resource and a boost to rural and urban economies. Some barbel fisheries are now providing jobs on and around former salmon fisheries which have gone to the wall owing to declining stocks and catches. The Hampshire Avon, Dorset Stour, Severn and Wye spring to mind as examples. Angling, both coarse and game, often plays an important economic role in the rural communities.

New barbel fisheries ?

So far, no barbel have been recorded in Scotland or Ireland but the fact that the species is now produced readily by fish farmers indicates that the potential for widespread stocking is very much with us. Also, we are told, climate change is likely to improve conditions in the British Isles for the warmth-loving barbel, perhaps with a central European summer climate and regular mild winter floods for southern Britain. In warmer future times the distribution of barbel could potentially be advanced well to the north.

Official permission to stock barbel into new river systems will not, however, be a foregone conclusion - game fishing interests, for instance, have concerns over barbel eating salmon and trout eggs and fry in the early spring. Whether this occurs widely or has a significant impact on salmonid stocks is unknown. Some salmon river keepers have not waited to find out and have no compunction in removing as many barbel as they can from waters under their stewardship. On chalk or clay-bedded rivers, barbel will often be living right on top of salmon spawning areas but in spatier upland systems most barbel probably occupy lower main river habitats, far downstream of major trout, sea trout and salmon spawning areas. Impacts on young salmonids through predation by barbel, if they occur at all, will, therefore, differ widely between river systems. Where rivers have a particularly high conservation value and have been designated as Special Areas of Conservation (SACs) partly on the basis of their salmon stocks, the introduction of barbel into new stretches may be refused because of concerns over potential impacts on the salmon population. The Wye and Hampshire Avon are good examples of this situation.

Where barbel and salmonids mix, it is quite possible that batches of salmon and trout eggs incubating under a few inches of gravel are temping and accessible to a hungry and determined barbel, especially in a mild spring. Emerging salmonid fry may also be easy meat for both chub and barbel, often predatory after the energy-sapping winter months. Introduced barbel must also compete to some extent for invertebrate food with both salmonid and coarse fish native to given river systems. Barbel thrive in good quality habitat and populations can amount to around half the total weight of fish present in suitable types of river; the species has the potential to dominate fish communities.

Predation and competition are joined by a third possibility of problems with introduced barbel - parasites and disease. For instance, it seems that introductions of barbel into the Hampshire Avon and Dorset Stour from the River Kennet in the 1950s brought the parasitic hook worm *Pomphorhynchus laevis* to these rivers. This lead to heavy infestations of these debilitating gut parasites, particularly in chub and also roach, dace and other species which eat shrimps, the parasite's intermediate host. There were widespread reports of lank, ill-conditioned Avon chub thought to be carrying high parasite burdens after barbel were stocked. This caused great concern at the time amongst keen Avon chub anglers. In the longer term, however, things have settled down and both the Avon and Stour are, once more, regularly producing well-conditioned six pound chub with a few sevens and one or two eight pounders - very big chub indeed.

Clearly, despite the pleasing prospect for barbel anglers of new northern river fisheries, developed initially through stocking, great care will be needed in deciding where the species will officially be allowed to spread in future. Of course, some anglers will be tempted take the law into their own hands and stock fish without permission, but this really isn't a good idea. As noted above, introduced species can have many unforeseen and damaging consequences, despite the overall success of many well known barbel fisheries which were started by stocking. Remember, it is a legal requirement to obtain Salmon & Freshwater Fishery Act, Section 30 consent from the Environment Agency before introducing fish in England and Wales. The Fishery Action Plans currently under development by the Agency will be an opportunity for the pros and cons of stocking to be debated by all interested parties at local river catchment level. If you have local knowledge and views on how best your river fishery should be maintained, improved or developed, throw in your 'ten pennoth' and take part in the consultation process.

Still water barbel.

Barbel can survive, but not breed in many still waters. Whether it is ethical to stock them under such conditions is a vexing question to which there are no right or wrong answers, just opinions. Given the choice, I would keep barbel in rivers where they can complete a normal life cycle and produce self-sustaining fisheries. That's the ecologist's viewpoint.

It is undeniably the case, however, that in some lakes at least, barbel survive and grow well, providing enjoyment for many anglers. Barbel are adaptable and can live in a range of conditions - from fast flowing rivers to cool reservoirs and even to warmer shallower lakes. Also, other species of fish unlikely to breed successfully in still waters (eg chub, brown trout, grass carp) are routinely stocked into ponds and lakes, so perhaps barbel shouldn't necessarily be regarded as a river-only species.

Farmed barbel grown in sluggish currents may already be acclimated to warm water with relatively low dissolved oxygen concentrations and may suffer little stress when placed in lakes. Wild river barbel transferred directly to warm lakes from cool well-oxygenated rivers, on the other hand, can experience real trauma. Not only may they feel 'short of breath' in the short term, but they will have been moved from a complex river habitat which they know intimately to a relatively featureless freshwater 'sea' with differing food resources, cover, competitors and unknown potential predators -

somewhat disorientating, to say the least. Barbel are rumoured to have been transferred illegally to lakes from a number of well known river fisheries - these fish are likely to suffer stress, lose condition and some may well die. Quite apart from the legal and ethical viewpoints - such fish movements are asking for trouble from fish welfare, public relations, disease and parasite perspectives too.

Barbel biology

Our British barbel, *Barbus barbus* is a member of the Cyprinidae (carp family of fishes) and is beautifully adapted to life in fast water. The powerful cylindrical body is streamlined to minimise drag, the large pectoral fins can be angled to press the fish onto the river bed where the flattened belly rests easily. The upper lobe of the tail is larger than the lower, angling the nose downward in normal swimming. As Fred Crouch has pointed out in his excellent book (Understanding Barbel), the humped back of a barbel will tend to cause the body to lift as water flows over the fish's nose and along its back. This is similar to the lift generated by an aircraft wing. The barbel has the ability to balance this lift against its angled pectoral and pelvic fins which produce down-forces. The down-force of the tail fin combines with that of the paired belly fins to enable the fish to hold position against the current with minimal effort. Just like a salmon parr, trout or dace, barbel ride fast currents as efficiently as possible, minimising their energy expenditure.

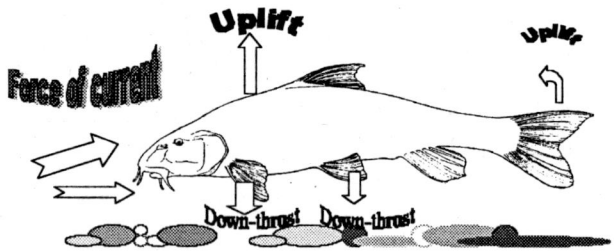

Barbel are also masters at sheltering from the main force of the current by using features such as rocks, cobbles, weed beds, dead wood snags and root masses, depressions in the river bed, bridge supports, etc. In such places food items are 'sucked in' behind boulders and similar obstructions to flow, creating natural larders in slack water areas - an ideal situation for this energy-conscious fish.

Where a 'crease' (fast water next to relative calm) is formed, many fish species, including barbel, chub and trout will tend to hold station in the calm water on the edge of the current, waiting to venture out into the flow to intercept any passing morsel. Barbel typically patrol in small shoals which push upstream to investigate a source of food (for instance bait-droppered hemp or maggots), circling back periodically with the current until they gain enough confidence to return upstream and feed at a new location away from their normal secure cover. For successful fishing it is often important to let the fish settle on the bait before angling for them.

Where barbel have been actively feeding a gravel bed appears pale and clean ('polished'), so thorough is the search for food. The pointed snout is perfect for foraging in crevices and weed beds, ploughing through gravel and rooting around under stones. Gravel beds teem with minnows, bullheads, stone loach, caddis larvae, shrimps, insect nymphs, midge larvae, tiny worms and little mussels. Silty areas have snails, alderfly, caddis and other larvae, shrimps, worms, small fish and algae - more potential barbel food. The two pairs of fleshy barbules are super-sensitive to smells and vibrations, allowing the sensing of food on and within the river bed. Although barbel can see well, they don't have to hunt food visually, as they can smell or feel it. The mouth is placed back from the snout, ideal for picking over river beds, sucking in invertebrates and small fish, etc whilst carefully filtering out unwanted items such as sticks and stones...lines and hooks.

Barbel will turn upside-down to hoover the underside of rock overhangs and logs and often suck snails from weed beds, sometimes feeding right at the surface, 'clooping' and 'tenting' like carp. Here's an evocative quote from Patrick Chalmers, writing in the early 1930s:

> *'In the quiet comes a croaking, then a chorus of small, snoring, puffing grunts. These noises are the barbel singing on the moonlit shallows because of their summer joie de vivre. They raise their blunt and bearded noses to the surface and above it. And I suppose the sound they make is caused by some outblowing of air. But, like the nightingale's, it is a song of summer and the velvet dark'.*

These fish are, then, adaptable feeders, foraging with few problems under a wide range of conditions. At the back of the throat (the pharynx) there are three paired rows of hooked grinding pharyngeal teeth which work against a horny pad on the roof of the mouth. This grinding mill breaks up tough food items which are then swallowed. These teeth are responsible for clean 'bite-offs' by fish like barbel, chub and carp when a hook length passes too far into the back of the throat.

Barbel senses in more detail.

Vision.

From underwater, the reflection of low-angle light off the water surface reduces a fish's 'cone of vision' to 97 degrees (the so-called 'Snell's window'). Deeper-lying fish can see furthest onto the bank - the closer a fish is to the surface, the more restricted its peripheral vision outside the water. A barbel or chub finning just sub-surface will only see a bread crust at the last minute whilst a deep-lying fish will see it (or you) coming some distance away.

Outside of the fish's circular overhead window of vision, the underside of the water surface acts as a mirror, reflecting objects underwater. It is difficult for us to visualise what a fish sees, but it could be akin to a circular central field (the window) which includes things outside and on the water, surrounded by a mirror reflection of the stream bed and underwater objects. At the same time the fish can see anything underwater in its direct sideways line of sight. Those unblinking eyes continuously monitor visual information, keeping the alert brain informed about the outside world.

Because barbel lying in mid-stream on the river bed can see furthest onto the banks, and because this is where they often are, it is critical to stay low and out of sight when approaching your swim and when fishing. Conversely, barbel tucked under a bank by your feet must rely on vibrations to detect your presence - they are pretty good at that too and so keeping quiet is also a good move. To a barbel you may appear or feel as dangerous as a heron or otter - the fish won't take any chances. Any sign of danger and barbel will lie doggo.

The barbel is equipped to feed at night or in turbid, silty conditions with no problem, sight will be unimportant at such times - smell, texture and vibrations will communicate all it needs to know. In clearer water, however, barbel undoubtedly have excellent vision and can pick out fast-moving minnows or tiny food items drifting in the current - trotted hemp seed, for instance. I know a chap who stayed on one evening rather later than he should on a certain stretch of the Dorset Stour, being rewarded with a big barbel which took fast-trotted bread flake in near darkness. Very adaptable fish are barbel.

Vibration/sound/hearing.

Izaak Walton advised anglers *'to be patient and forbear swearing, lest they be heard'*.

Most anglers I know swear quite freely, especially after missing a barbel bite. Whilst we hear well and can feel vibrations through the soles of our feet or fingertips, fish pick up tiny pressure changes through their body tissues/swim bladder and inner ears and, particularly, through their lateral lines. This allows fish to 'feel' at a distance. Sound waves travel nearly five times faster in water than in air. If a hydrophone (water-tight microphone) is lowered into a pool, even we humans can hear gentle footsteps approaching. It takes more energy to propagate sound waves underwater than in air but, once they are moving, they travel a long way with little loss of information; in this way whales 'sing' long-distance to each other under the sea. The noise generated by an underwater explosion can be detected half-way round the world. The background noise under a calm sea has the same sound level as a typical human conversation a yard away, in a rough sea or weir pool, the background noise is equivalent to a small propeller-driven aircraft ! Jaques Cousteau's silent world was not well-named.

Fish listen-in to this barrage of noise in several ways. The lateral line system, which extends from the tail right up and over the head, picks up the direction and presence of low-frequency (deep) sounds. These would include a foot-fall or water currents set up, for instance, by a cormorant or large pike swimming quickly towards them. This system works best at ranges within 20 feet. The lateral line can also pick up higher-frequency vibrations as can the inner ear and air-filled swim bladder, but cannot detect the direction from which these sounds come. The fish inner-ear system works best on sounds coming from a range of 30 feet plus. Compared with our ears, fish only respond to relatively low-frequency sounds. An angler's conversation will mostly (99%) reflect off the water surface, but a heavy footfall, shuffled chair or bank stick hammered into a bank will transmit strong vibrations to the ever-sensitive lateral lines 'listening' below.

A further clever property of the lateral line system is that it can detect turbulent flows and eddies, making it a superb aid to finding and taking up residence in sheltered lies, away from the buffeting flows of the main stream. The lateral line canals on the head may also be important for homing in on prey, especially under low-light conditions. It is impossible for us humans to understand just how a fish's senses allow it to perceive the world but we can be sure that fish are well tapped in to all available information which could improve their chances of survival. Barbel can often outsmart us just by being aware of our presence or detecting our fishing tackle. Fish don't have to be clever to avoid capture, just wary. They also learn quickly from frightening experiences…..such as being caught.

Few anglers bother to approach or fish their swims with stealth - why, I do not understand. Also, (and this can be very frustrating for careful fishermen), you may have crept up to your swim like a panther, baited it up ready for the evening, sitting quiet as a heron, only to have some berk in a dayglo orange tee shirt stomp up to the edge of the bank, peering into the river asking 'Had any luck mate?' The start of the bad luck was him turning up.

Taste/smell

> *'But timorous Barbels will not taste the bit*
> *Till with their tayles they have unhooked it,*
> *And all the baytes the Fisher can devise*
> *Cannot beguile their warie jealousies'*
>
> Guillaume de Saluste du Bartas, in 'La Semaine' (1578)

Our senses of taste and smell are separate whilst those of fish are probably effectively combined - sensing dissolved chemicals. Barbel pick up chemical information with the nostrils, barbules, surface of the chin/belly and fins, the tongue and inside of the mouth. A catfish can have as many as 100,000 'taste buds' on its body surface, mostly on the barbules, allowing it to smell food or danger drifting on the current or food hiding in the gravel below. I don't know how many taste buds barbel have but they are probably pretty well endowed in this department. Take a close look at the photographs of the barbel's mouth to see the bumpy skin all over the lips and barbules, which are like your tongue - a highly sensitive chemical detection system covered in taste buds.

Absolutely tiny concentrations of some chemicals can be detected. When the skin of a minnow is damaged, by a pike or heron, for instance, specialised cells release a chemical called 'alarm substance' which seems to cause other shoal members to flee. Maybe other cyprinid fish, such as barbel and carp also possess this or similar chemical warning systems, allowing communication between shoal members. This may be one of the protective benefits of evolving as a shoaling species - warning each other of danger.

Salmon can detect the smell of mammal skin at very low levels - an adaptation primarily helping them avoid predatory seals and bears. Even the smell of our hands is reported to cause salmon to turn around on a fish ladder and race back downstream. Smell your hands - even we can detect these chemicals. Mammalian skin secretes a substance called alpha-serine and some people have smellier skin than others. Alpha-serine may be a trigger to fishes' innate fright behaviour. Whether barbel have similar worries to salmon I don't know but touching baits with unwashed hands could well be a bad move. By developing the habit of washing your hands with river water well downstream from your swim before baiting up, you may be tipping the odds in your favour. Why not try using a plastic bag to avoid touching your bait - it could make a difference to your success.

All fish with barbules can sense very low levels of dissolved chemicals and use this ability both to find food and to warn them of danger. Lab experiments with catfish have shown that they aren't frightened of all human smells - saliva, for instance, is the third most attractive solution tested (after worms and liver). Again, whether cyprinids react in similar ways I don't know. Maybe there's scope for chewing up your cheese paste.

Cyprinids such as carp and barbel are very sensitive to and attracted to amino acids, the building blocks of proteins. This may be why barbel and carp love meaty or trout pellet pastes, luncheon meat, garlic sausage, meat balls, etc - they are programmed to respond to muscle-building food. Barbel taste buds help them sort and select food particles from a mouthful of sediment sucked up from the river bed. Inedible bits are ejected through the gills or spat out through the mouth. Fish can both suck and blow with great force and very quickly indeed. Barbel will spit out a hook bait instantly they feel anything wrong with it. These fish are very sophisticated feeders, with tremendous ability to detect any suspicious aspects of bait or terminal tackle. No wonder barbel bites can be so hard to come by on heavily fished waters - crude end rigs and well-used baits are probably readily recognised and may be rejected as being just too risky. Getting barbel feeding confidently before casting a bait can be a very important tactic. Cast too soon to spooky fish and you may wait a long time for that first bite. Get them feeding actively, however, and the playing of fish in the swim won't put off a shoal of barbel which are confidently on the feed.

Also, angling technique can be all-important. A downstream-legered bait will cause a barbel to pull against the tension of the rod - increasing the chances of rejection but a well-balanced upstream leger will move down with the current as a fish mouths the bait, creating minimal resistance and increasing the chance of a committed bite. Upstream legering is well worth a go. Alternatively, holding a loop of line which you can gently release when downstream legering reduces pressure on the end rig and can inspire more confidence in a wary barbel.

The fact that barbel tend generally to remain in tip-top condition means, of course, that angling pressure doesn't stop them feeding - they are just cute enough to avoid food with hooks inside. Some fish may well be more gullible than others. This is known to be true on fisheries where individual barbel can be recognised. In this sense, barbel are a form of river carp - a close relative renowned for its ability to evade capture by all but the most skilled and patient anglers. Some carp are much smarter and caught less often than others. Some big carp and barbel may never be caught again, once they have learnt from a few mistakes as young fish. Other fish can go for years without making a mistake but then be caught by a skilful fisherman.

Learning to survive

Survival is everything to wild animals, they are born with basic instincts helping them avoid early dangers. Experience gained as they grow is honed and built upon as animals learn through life. Fish are able to learn quickly and combine this ability with their inherited anti-predator behaviour. Getting caught is an experience which barbel are likely to try and avoid in future. Maybe it's a scare similar to a close encounter with a predator or maybe it is less intense than that - I don't know. What is obvious is that catch-and-release of barbel and similar fish can't be too damaging as they survive it on a regular basis and remain healthy. But they do learn from the experience. Only a happy, relaxed barbel will feed confidently which means that you often need to think carefully about presenting new baits or to use new approaches to stay one step ahead of the fish - easier said than done. Chapter 5 explores this topic further.

Camouflage and barbel behaviour

The barbels' colouration is a wonderful blend of dark metallic brown / green on the head and back, copper / gold on the flanks and creamy yellow / white on the belly. The fins are orange / coral pink blending to grey / white. Underwater these beautiful fish just vanish against their background. Barbel drift like ghosts over a gravel bed, blending in so well that only a moving fin may draw your eye, the rest of the fish materialising as you tune in to underwater forms. Any predator looking in from above, be it a heron, or osprey will have similar difficulty in seeing barbel. Underwater predators such as otters, mink, cormorants and pike are combated by the fish's counter-shaded body - darker on top, light underneath. With sunlight filtering down from above the dark back balances with the paler belly and intermediate flanks to 'dissolve' the fish into its background. This is why virtually all fish have dark backs and pale bellies - except cave fish which live in darkness, have no eyes and are pale all over.

© Clare Yates

Prickly customers

The barbel's dorsal and anal fins have sharp serrated tips which help protect young fish from being swallowed by predators - including bigger barbel. These spiny fin rays also get tangled up in soft-meshed landing and keep nets so beware and look after your fish - only netting them when necessary. Barbel don't do well in poorly designed landing or keep nets. Split fins can heal up quickly but are best avoided. The physical protection afforded by spines becomes less important as the fish grow large - by then they have developed a wealth of experience and few predators are big enough to eat an adult barbel. But big barbel can't realise how big they are in relation to predators and so remain wary all their lives of even the smallest threats. If they take a chance, it could be their last.

Don't underestimate the caution of these fish if you want to catch them at all regularly. I just can't understand why, despite this basic understanding of how a fish is likely to feel, so many anglers stride along the edge of the bank, crash down their tackle boxes and shout to their mates that they have seen a shoal of barbel....rest assured, the barbel will have seen and heard them too!

No place like home

Barbel learn the local geography of their home range, knowing where safe cover is, where food is abundant, where the current makes it hard work to keep station and where undulations in the bed, boulders, tree roots, etc deflect the current, creating energy-efficient lies. In a world of constant movement which the fish has to battle against, learning to use the current to your advantage is immensely important. Less energy spent fighting the current means that less feeding time is needed to replace that energy. Feeding often means exposure on gravel shallows which could be dangerous. Barbel will minimise both danger and unnecessary energy expenditure, making sure that as much energy as possible is available for growth and reaching maturity. This is why, where food is relatively plentiful, barbel spend most of their time hiding under banks or logs - it's safe there!

Barbel may be found singly or in groups of various sizes. Being part of a shoal may bring benefits, both in terms of 'safety in numbers' and in sharing the task of finding food in a varied environment. Perhaps there is more chance of finding an abundant patch of shrimps, bloodworm or caddis larvae if many mouths are probing the river bed - the whole shoal can then move in and benefit from the find. Maybe surface 'rolling' behaviour signals the finding of a good food source, communicating it to other members of the shoal. Certainly, it is common to see barbel and other shoaling cyprinids (roach, tench, bream, crucians and other carp) 'head-and-tailing' as the light falls and bites are expected - these fish seem to be actively on the feed.

We understand very little of the complex social behaviour of freshwater fish. Evolutionary success means staying alive long enough to produce as many viable offspring as possible. The barbel's life cycle is adapted to this end - it pays us anglers to understand the biological background which programmes this behaviour. If we begin to appreciate what makes these fish tick, we may stand a better chance of catching a few.

Vitally important to barbel of all sizes is, of course, staying alive. The chance of a meal to a fish is unlikely to weigh heavily against a risk of danger. Fish can do without food much more easily than us; being cold-blooded, they don't have to burn any fuel to stay warm. Fish can also stop growing for long periods, just 'ticking over' on available resources. Growth may resume if and when conditions improve. Therefore, in everyday life, feeding is only really likely to happen when barbel have little or no suspicion of danger. Carp behave similarly unless in such crowded waters that intense competition for food forces them to feed. For barbel in natural waters it will always be better to stay in cover and not to risk feeding out in the open if anything has happened in the recent past to scare fish.

Barbel guru Stuart Morgan has cleverly used this basic fact to devise a very successful approach to catching shy barbel. He spends a good deal of time walking the banks looking for fish and noting carefully where barbel are seen. Then, over a few days, Stuart baits up a secluded area upstream of the barbel's daytime cover, often using carefully formulated John Baker pastes and boilies. He does not fish either the daytime refuge or the pre-baited areas, allowing the barbel to gain confidence. When observations have shown the routes which the barbel take to travel from cover to their feeding areas, Stuart places a paste or boilie bait in their path and sits back to await action around dusk. This is clever because the barbel have become used to eating the particular bait but have had no chance to associate being caught with the area where they find the hook bait - so they take it confidently. See John Baker's 'Modern barbel baits & tactics' for further information.

Barbel, then, survive by using their immensely well-tuned senses, stealth, experience and via their body shape, moulded by natural selection for efficient use of flowing waters. In the tough world of Nature, individuals which don't measure up don't survive to breed and pass on their genes to the next generation. Success breeds success. To catch specimen fish, (which are old and wise), regularly you need to be able to get around this set of refined senses and present an acceptable bait naturally enough to lull them into a false sense of security. Then, as a conscientious angler, you have to play, land and release your fish essentially unharmed. Stealth plus watercraft and skill equal success - and some people think there's no challenge in angling!

What makes a good barbel swim ?

Big barbel like to rest in safe cover in pools next to a fast run where they can feed at dusk and during the night. Smooth, medium-depth glides with current speeds of brisk walking pace, clean gravel beds and close to safe hiding places are the basic habitat requirements.

Intensive observations of barbel by specimen-hunting anglers show that - on clear-watered rivers, at least - groups of barbel tend to live in particular stretches for long periods of time. If you get it right you can catch several fish, often of a similar size, at a sitting. Very often, barbel will have seen/smelt and inspected your bait dozens of times during a fishing session whilst you may not have detected a single tremor of a bite. I'm sure that this happens all the time and sometimes wonder how we manage to catch any barbel at all, so good are these fish at detecting whether a potential food item is behaving naturally, or not. On some rivers with low angling pressure many unusual baits may simply not be recognised by the fish as food. If barbel have spent their whole lives seeking out small shrimps, snails, caddis larvae, nymphs and worms why should they suddenly fancy wolfing down a Campbell's meat ball, for instance? Pre-baiting to accustom fish to novel baits can be critically important to success. Alternatively, using something natural for bait which the fish are already used to eating isn't a bad move either - see Chapter 5.

As all estate agents will tell you, location is the key to a desirable residence. Barbel would agree. Despite appearances, many superficially attractive swims seldom harbour barbel - often they just don't seem to have read the books. Both individual fish and shoals probably routinely move around over a few hundred metres (the distance depending on the sort of river they are living in and the quality of the habitat), exploiting different food-rich patches in sequence; you need to go looking for the fish. Sometimes you will catch a flash of white belly as food is taken in mid-water, golden flashes from the flanks can signal fish feeding actively over gravel. Barbel tenting for snails in crowfoot beds or rolling at dusk are well worth looking out for too. Rolling barbel are feeding barbel.

Despite the obvious value of fish location, few anglers look for fish, most chosing to fish blind, sitting it out in the belief that barbel are in the swim and will come onto the feed sooner or later. This may be true on well-known consistent swims but the feeding fish could just as easily be half a mile up- or down-stream. Nothing increases your chances of success more than having some fish there to catch!

Substantial angling pressure affects barbel behaviour profoundly, both by attracting fish with baits and ground bait and by scaring them away when individuals get caught too often. Where there is a big shoal and individual fish are not caught often, the group may stay in residence more or less permanently, despite frequent successful angling. On hard-fished stretches, however, the capture of a single fish from a shoal or even a clumsily presented familiar bait may cause a mass exodus to a safer swim with a good cover feature - a sunken log pile or undercut bank with overhead root masses, for instance. Crowfoot and bulrush beds are also favourite haunts, offering shelter from the current, shelter from danger and easily obtained food resources.

Barbel (and carp) also learn when most anglers go home - coming out to feed when the risk of capture is least. Night feeding may often be a response to daytime angling pressures. Sometimes, it's worth trying a huge bait at last knockings as many fishermen lob unused balls of paste or chunks of luncheon meat into the river at the end of the day. I've seen barbel caught on hard stretches of the Hampshire Avon on quarter-tins of Bacon Grill - that's an unusually big bait. Barbel also learn where it is dangerous to feed, so deliberately keeping off the well beaten angling track also pays dividends.

Barbel are able to become very discerning as to whether a tempting morsel of food contains a hook or is attached to a line. Wafting baits with their fins or blowing water at it allows the fish to distinguish free offerings from tethered baits. Long leaders and neutrally-buoyant rigs can help (see Chapter 5). Baits which provoke a fright response are termed 'blown' and their use is very counter-productive. This leads to a battle of wits using prolonged baiting up with novel baits, fine tackle and clever rigs to outwit wary fish. See Roger Miller's 'The complete barbel angler', Tony Miles & Trefor Wests' 'Quest for barbel' and John Bakers book for detailed good advice. Wary barbel contrast completely with the relative ease with which you can catch fish on quieter waters, underlining the ability of these fish to learn by experience. On popular fisheries, just taking the trouble to walk as far away from the car park as possible and choosing swims which most other anglers avoid can make a big difference to catches. Don't follow the crowd - after all, they have conditioned the barbel to avoid what most people do. Go barbel spotting on out of the way stretches and try to develop novel approaches to catching these challenging fish.

Competition for food

A further factor in barbel angling success lies in the richness of differing river types. In the placid chalk streamy Hampshire Avon where the bed is alive with shrimps and caddis larvae, competition for food may be low and barbel can afford to be choosy when selecting a meal. Amid the rich wet meadows, each rain storm ensures a ready supply of big fat wandering lobworms and slugs, just right for a chub or barbel snack. Contrast this with thin, poor upland soils where worms are few and far between. In a more rugged upland situation with fast, energy-sapping, turbulent flows and a relatively sparse invertebrate food supply, a trickle of maggots may represent an opportunity too good to miss. I'm pretty sure that this makes some rivers far easier to catch barbel from than others. Rivers with dense shoals of medium-sized barbel are also likely to be more productive than those with fewer, larger fish. Competition for food within shoals can effectively make fish take chances - if they don't eat it another fish will.

Reading barbel and chub rivers

© MGN Ltd

Barbel will often hold up in a secure lie during the day, this may be in a bridge or weir pool, a smaller hole in the river bed, under a thick crowfoot bed, amongst a 'cabbage patch', behind true bulrush stands, in log piles or below boulders, under tree roots, bushes, scum rafts or undercut banks. Shoals of fish drift gently around when undisturbed - you can see them if you take the trouble to look. Some people are better at seeing fish than others but you can greatly improve your chances with practice. Once you have your 'eye-in', you are away and wonder why you found it so hard to see fish in the first place.

The best way to find barbel-holding features is to go 'polaroiding', walking the fishery slowly upstream under clear-water conditions with the sun shining over your shoulder and noting all likely lies and any fish spotted. A note book comes in handy. Barbel blend into a gravel-bedded background extremely well, but may give their presence away by surface rolling, flashing over the gravel, flicking a large red pectoral fin or a gently waving tail. Keep low, walk lightly, shield your eyes with a brimmed hat or cap and take your time. Also, consider climbing a few trees, getting in with some chest waders, swimming trunks or even a SCUBA tank; it is surprising how much more you learn when you are actually in or over the river. Time spent fish-watching is seldom wasted, it's good fun too. But be careful when climbing, wading or swimming - nasty accidents can happen in swift cool rivers.

Life in the fast lane

Reading the water requires experience. A major factor in fish distribution is current speed. In a study of East Anglian rivers, Richard Smith discovered that where mills impound the water, ponding it back upstream, far fewer chub were found in likely looking spots than downstream in the mill streams where the current is brisker. On the River Wensum an average current speed of 20 cm per second supported, on average, less than 10 chub per 200 metre section, a 40 cm per second current 40 chub on average whilst a 60 cm per second flow often yielded 40 to 50 chub. Perhaps the current speed determines how much drifting food, on average, goes past a fish's nose each day and thus how many chub a given section of river can feed. In slow currents there might be strong competition for the meagre fare and vice versa.

© Clare Yates

It is quite likely that barbel respond to habitat quality in similar ways but we don't know since so little detailed research work on barbel has been done. This is surprising, given the popularity of the species and is something that the Barbel Society, amongst others, is trying to change.

Good and bad breeding seasons

Another factor of major importance to river chub and barbel stocks is the relationship between warm summers and good breeding years. Hot summers, such as some of those of the mid 1970s and late 1980s gave rise to strong year classes of fry which, in turn produced sizeable shoals of surviving fish. These shoals show up in a fishery for many years with numbers gradually dwindling and average sizes increasing. Stocks can be dominated for a long time by fish produced during just one or two hot summers. Warm years also promote growth in coarse fish generally and an overall pattern of rapid growth can be seen in fish from rivers in differing parts of the country after a good summer. Barbel may live up to 30+ years or even more under favourable conditions and so a long-lived individual should, on average, get a chance to spawn in at least some good years.

Of course, a run of cool summers (not unknown in the UK) may give rise to poor recruitment and a 'hole' in the fish stocks for several seasons; this is a situation where stocking can be a worthwhile proposition. Similarly, where there is a severe shortage of suitable gravel spawning shallows because of extensive dredging or chronic siltation problems causing most incubating eggs to die, stocking may be a necessity. When the fluctuating fortunes of coarse fish species in a given river are understood, for instance, after regular electro-fishing surveys or through analysis of angler catch records, it may be possible to obtain suitable healthy stock fish to fill in gaps in the population age structure. In this way, the performance of the fishery can be evened out over a number of years.

Where fish spawn successfully in most years, stocking is unlikely to be worthwhile - self-sustaining fish stocks, whilst not always attainable, are a sound management objective.

When introducing fish of any species it is far better to obtain local stock, if at all possible, so as to try to make sure that the newly-planted fish will be well adapted to the fishery. Make sure that suitable habitat is available for stocked fish - don't just put them in and hope for the best. Remember that barbel raised in slowly-flowing fish farm tanks, for instance, have a nasty shock if turned out into a fast-flowing cold river where they must suddenly battle against the current and where the regular pelleted feed which they have grown up on is no longer available. These fish have to learn quickly to find and recognise natural food, catch and eat it. By no means all stocked fish can adapt to conditions in the wild and many are likely to die. Choose stock fish and their suppliers carefully - don't introduce parasitised or diseased fish - get them checked out and do buy fish which are fit enough to survive the rigours of life in your fishery. Farmed barbel, for instance, can be conditioned to faster current speeds before stocking out, improving their chances of survival.

The appliance of science - barbel of the Severn

To really understand what makes fisheries tick you need to get some good quality applied science underway. P.C.Hunt and J.W.Jones from Liverpool University started the barbel ball rolling with some pioneering research on the River Severn in the early 1970s.

The Severn is immense, being 325km from its mid-Wales source to the sea and with a catchment of 70,000 square kilometres. Hunt and

Jones' study was based on the 24km section between Norton in Shropshire and Arley in Worcestershire, here, the river is 25-55 metres wide with pools of up to 10 metres depth, even in summer. Floods can add 4 metres to the depth - this is no sedate chalk stream. Summer current speeds of up to 1.2 metres per second, coupled with a gravelly / sandy bed with stands of crowfoot and milfoil and milling invertebrate populations provide fine barbel habitat and good fishing.

During the study barbel were electric-fished monthly between May 1971 and September 1972 - a series of short sections was chosen for study and individual fish were :

- Measured (tip of snout to tail fork - 'fork length') and accurately weighed,
- Aged - scale samples (from the 'shoulder' area) removed,
- Tagged - either on a gill cover or on the dorsal fin.

Information on fish numbers, population biology, growth and movements was analysed, written up and published (see papers in reading list). It is worth mentioning, in passing, that electric-fishing needs Environment Agency consent in England and Wales and must be done with safe gear by people who know what they are doing, otherwise more harm than good can be done, both to fish and people. Water and electricity can be a deadly combination - be careful.

Some key results from Hunt and Jones' major study are as follows. Big barbel were typically found in deep gravelly runs with over-hanging bank side vegetation - a classic barbel habitat. In winter barbel shoals were located in deeper more sluggish water than in summer.

Of the 3122 barbel tagged during the study, 531 were recaptured either by anglers or by electric fishing. 92 tagged barbel were recaptured downstream from where they were tagged, 152 upstream and 287 at the same site. Anglers helped a great deal with the study by reporting captures of tagged fish but some removed tags, probably where these were causing damage. Modern plastic tags are much better and can be used with few ill effects but, back in the 1970s, metal tags often led to fungal infections and sores. Nobody could blame anglers for removing them from fish which were suffering.

The Severn barbel population in the study area was comprised of a large component (86%) which stayed within a 5km 'home range' and a roving component with individuals travelling up to 54 km from their site of tagging. The bigger the barbel, the greater the tendency to move around in the river system. Tagged barbel often moved, especially after floods. These fish do not find it easy to battle strong currents and may often be displaced downstream in high flows. Just before the main study the climate was, at times, very wet. In mid-July 1968 there were severe floods and the spawning that year produced virtually no surviving young barbel - perhaps all the fry were swept away or maybe the eggs were silted, or temperatures were too low for fry survival. Some adult fish were caught in salmon traps in the estuary showing just how far downstream floods can sweep barbel - the species is well adapted to fast water habitats but they don't have it all their own way. After the 1968 spawning failure the growth rate of surviving barbel increased - maybe competition for food had decreased.

Tagged barbel were sometimes recaptured in groups, indicating that shoals tend to stay together, especially around the spring breeding migration. Spawning took place in May, June and early July. Other fish appeared to be 'loners'. One barbel was caught by the same angler in the same swim on five independent occasions over a period of two months. And this in a river the size of the Severn !

Scales taken from 7071 barbel showed that the annual growth check was laid down in May when the fish spawned. Growth didn't stop in winter although it was much slower than in summer. Growth is quickest from June to September, slows towards November and there is virtually no length increase from December to June although body condition does tend to improve over winter. Catches of known big barbel through the year commonly show winter weight gains of one to two pounds; much of this may be due to gorging on worms and maturing eggs. Remember, all leviathans are female.

Severn water temperatures were rarely below 15 degrees Celsius from June to September - barbel grow fastest in warm weather. Barbel older than 8 years became increasingly more difficult to age because of the tiny increases in scale diameter as the older fish grew very little in length. Females grew faster than males after an age of four years and ultimately grow into the biggest fish. All record barbel are female. There was a greater preponderance of males amongst younger fish and females amongst older fish. The overall sex ratio was 2.41 males to each female. Most fish were sexed whilst in spawning condition - the sexes are indistinguishable externally for the rest of the year.

In September 1971 the river was closed for fishing for one week prior to 'The National' fishing match, exactly at this time virtually all barbel showed a cessation in growth! This shows that, at least in the 1970s (and probably still), angler's baits / ground bait are a very important source of food for Severn barbel. I'm sure this is true on other rivers too and for many fish species. This study has taught us so much about Severn barbel - wouldn't it be good to see more population studies on other barbel rivers so that we can begin to understand how typical these results are? Modern methods of tracking fish are opening up new possibilities.

Radio-tracking barbel on the River Nidd

Martyn Lucas of the University of Durham, has done some very interesting research on barbel behaviour in Yorkshire's River Nidd. He implanted radio transmitters into the body cavity of 31 barbel (the fish healed up well), released them and was then able to locate individual fish on their differing radio frequencies over the course of the following year or so. Fish can either be located on foot by walking the river bank with a directional antenna or via a set of 'listening stations' which are set up at intervals along the river and which allow automatic recordings to be stored for later retrieval - clever stuff. The results are fascinating.

Barbel moved considerable distances, from between 2km to nearly 20km, four fish moved out of the River Nidd altogether and into the main Yorkshire Ouse. Even relatively low weirs clearly restricted the movement of barbel attempting to move upstream to spawn. This may well be a problem in many lowland rivers where fish of several species need to migrate to find suitable spawning habitats but are impeded by sluices or weirs. Coarse fish passes would help in this respect and research is underway to design suitable structures. Funding their widespread construction is another challenge for The Environment Agency.

Nidd barbel have an annual migration, upstream in spring (May) to spawn on shallow gravel bars and then back downstream during the summer. Females move back downstream more quickly than males after spawning. In autumn and winter both sexes are displaced downstream by high flows - just as on the Severn.

Barbel have a daily behavioural cycle with peak feeding activity in summer early in the morning and late in the evening. In winter fish were far less active than in summer (around 20% of peak summer levels) with a single peak of feeding activity around dusk.

Barbel activity levels at all times of year were directly related to water temperature, lowest below 5 degrees C and highest above 15 degrees C. Barbel mainly stayed close to cover during the day - under overhanging willows, tucked into root masses or weed beds and close to rapid currents, but ranged more widely under cover of darkness. During the study five of the tagged barbel were caught by anglers and all were in good condition.

The River Meuse

Etienne Baras from the University of Liege, Belgium has, for many years, researched barbel ecology in the River Meuse catchment, concentrating particularly on the River Ourthe. These studies were set up following worries over the decline in barbel stocks on the Meuse, a river which has been subjected to extensive dredging, impoundment and pollution. Funding for the work was granted in recognition of the economic importance of Belgian barbel fisheries. In the 1980s many western European barbel stocks were recognised as being under threat from habitat destruction and over-fishing. The loss of barbel stocks was seen as being serious in such a commercially important species. Maybe our UK river coarse fisheries should be valued rather more highly when government grant-in-aid is allocated to the Environment Agency. Also, maybe some of the bigger clubs and associations could fund some barbel work of their own.

From 1973 to 1974 Baras followed the movements of 3000 tagged barbel through electric fishing surveys and anglers catch returns. Of 736 recaptured fish, 90% had moved less than 2km and less than 1% moved more than 8km from the place where they were originally tagged. Fish which were recaptured several times had an average home range of just over a kilometre of river.

What Baras really wanted to be able to do was to follow the day to day behaviour of individual fish. With improving technology he eventually did this, using radio-tracking methods on his beloved barbel in a study which spanned 1989 to 1991. 21 fish were implanted with transmitters, released and then regularly relocated by researchers wandering the river bank with antenna receivers. 40,000 individual fixes on barbel were recorded - that's dedication for you. And, interestingly, the individual barbel definitely showed home-range behaviour over stretches of river ranging from 75 metres to over 2 kilometres. During winter, summer and early autumn the home range of a barbel was restricted to its daily activity area. Within this area fish typically moved over 200 metres or so of river, staying in two key areas:

1. Shallow gravel feeding areas explored at dawn and dusk.
2. Residence areas (safe 'lies') which could be deeper gravel runs, pools, undercut banks or deadwood snags. When in these barbel can lie around for over 80% of the day apparently not doing anything….no wonder we often have to wait a long time for a bite.

Major movements did occur, however - either during floods when barbel were displaced downstream or during the annual spawning migration when fish could suddenly up and leave, travelling 12km or more to favoured spawning shallows. Overall, then, River Ourthe barbel in Belgium behaved in very similar ways to River Nidd and Severn barbel.

After being swept downstream by floods or after upstream breeding migrations, Ourthe barbel homed back to their original stretches of river. What really amazes me about Etienne Baras' study is that some of those fish which had travelled many kilometres were then able to home back to their old favourite lies with an accuracy of one or two metres. Just think, a fish will travel a round-trip of maybe tens of kilometres over a few days or weeks, returning back 'home' to slide under its old log or patch of tree roots. Imagine how well these fish must know the territory to be able to do that; it must be vitally important for them to get back to a patch which they know well, where they are safe and can find food.

Radio-tracking really can reveal some fascinating details of the behaviour of fish under natural conditions. It also gives you some impression of how devastating it must be to these fish to have a dredging team go through their stretch and rip out the cover which the fish have come to depend upon for security and the gravel bars where they traditionally find their food, spawn and live as juveniles.

Etienne Baras went on to do some neat experiments radio-tracking members of a barbel shoal, releasing them up- or down-stream from each other. When the barbel moved off to choose an area to re-settle, they always went for what we would recognise as good quality barbel habitat but not all suitable areas were selected. An important secondary requirement was the presence of other barbel, ideally a shoal of at least 10 fish. This is very interesting as it underlines that barbel often choose to live where they have access to cover, food and shoal members. Tracking of individual fish showed that barbel probably don't recognise each other - any other barbel seem to do as fellow shoal members.

The key importance of cover

On one occasion Baras needed some fish to tag, so he went to a one metre-deep pool with a sunken tree where there was dense cover over only two square metres of river bed - a dip with the electric fisher probe produced 34 barbel from that one spot. It makes you wonder just how often fish are packed like this into small areas of highly preferred habitat doesn't it? Successful barbel anglers stress just how important it is to get to know swims in detail, ideally watching which areas barbel use and where their normal travel lanes are.

It is reassuring to confirm that the general 'rules' for barbel behaviour, gleaned over the years by our best known barbel anglers are borne out by scientific studies. These principles of barbel activity are sketched out below:

1. On little-fished waters barbel may remain more active during the day than on more heavily fished rivers where dawn & dusk feeding periods are often the norm.
2. In summer barbel are far more active than during winter. Daily activity curves decline in cooler water and single dusk feeding periods seem usual in winter. Despite this, barbel generally gain weight in winter.

When fishing conditions are good - overcast, mild with some colour in the water, barbel feeding activity will generally be higher than in cold, clear water conditions, even on a heavily-fished water. Also, of course, careful ground-baiting can get a shoal feeding during the day and good bait presentation will further enhance your chances. Coloured water which cuts down light penetration may look to barbel like a prolonged twilight period and so reduce their caution. Floods wash in many worms, they flush out invertebrates from the river bed as it scours and they disorientate small fish which may then be vulnerable to predatory barbel. Many factors influence fishing success. It is unwise to be too dogmatic regarding fish behaviour, the words always and never don't apply to fishing. Barbel adapt their behaviour to suit local conditions, also they often do unpredictable things - that's what keeps it interesting.

More radio-tracking research work on barbel with fish from differing river types, would be very interesting and worthwhile. The more we understand about coarse fish ecology, the better we can conserve them and their habitats for the enjoyment of generations of anglers and naturalists to come.

Wildlife benefits of good fishery management

© Clare Yates

If we get the habitat right for barbel, many other species will benefit too. Gravel shallows which barbel must have for spawning can also harbour spawning salmon, trout, grayling, dace, lampreys, bullheads and beds of water crowfoot - all species in need of conservation. Overhanging bank side vegetation which shelters young barbel from the main current also provides a potential home for native crayfish amongst underwater roots and food for water voles along the river bank. Pools with undercut root masses provide safe cover for adult barbel, chub and other fish and, above water level, snug holts for otters.

Spawning behaviour

Female barbel produce from around 3,000 to 30,000 small (2mm) yellow eggs - the bigger the fish, the greater the annual investment in egg production. The eggs hatch after around 11 days at 14 degrees C and in 5-6 days at 19 degrees C. After hatching it takes around two weeks for the tiny larvae to absorb their remaining yolk sac and start finding food for themselves. Barbel larvae avoid strong light, hiding amongst the gravel. A rough river bed with plenty of cobbles and rocks is known to be favoured by these young fish. The rough bottom may help them evade predators such as chub and shelter from the main force of the current. Young barbel tend to stay close to shallow gravel-bedded areas where cover is plentiful.

Barbel are generally slow-growers in the UK where waters tend to be cool compared with central Europe. Sexual maturity is reached after three to five years. Nature has moulded the breeding behaviour so that females choose to spawn with healthy males to produce as many viable offspring as possible. The general lack of tiny barbel seen in most fisheries indicates that life is very tough for this species until it reaches a large enough size to escape most predators and to battle against strong currents. Once this testing early phase of life is survived, growing barbel can progressively move out into fast water habitats where they reign supreme amongst river-dwelling coarse fish. Chances of survival improve greatly after the critical early stages.

Observations of spawning barbel

During the spring of 1974 three fish biologists, R.S.Hancock, J.W.Jones and R.Shaw set out to follow the spawning migration and to observe the spawning behaviour of barbel in the clear chalk stream waters of the Yorkshire Wold's beautiful Driffield Beck. This stream has a pebble bottom, rich crowfoot beds, is around 15 metres wide with summer depths of up to 3 metres and, then, had thriving stocks wild brown trout and grayling.

Adult barbel are only year-round residents in the lower tidal part of the Beck below Hempholme lock, 12 km below the study site. They make the annual spawning migration to reach suitable habitat over this distance, a 25km round trip! Young barbel produced in the nursery areas progressively drop back down stream as they grow, ultimately recruiting into the adult population at the bottom of the fishery. This tells us a great deal about just how far barbel can be forced to travel in order to complete their life cycle even on a small stream and how intimately this is linked to adequate habitat quality. Where gravel shallows have been dredged out or bunged solid with silt, fish must travel further to find suitable breeding areas. On some rivers with histories of deep dredging and straightening, this will mean migrations of many miles. On some dredged sections between impassable weirs barbel may not get the chance to spawn at all.

Back in 1974 our three intrepid fish biologists erected hides next to the Driffield gravel shallows where barbel were known to spawn, sat back quietly and recorded their remarkable observations.

The key results from the study were as follows. Pre-spawning fish holed up in a pool below the gravel shallows in May with spawning being observed in June. No feeding behaviour was observed at this time and this is when the annual growth check appears on barbel scales. As an aside, it's worth noting that fishing for spawning barbel - even if you wanted to, which I hope you don't, - would probably be a waste of time, they have other things on their minds. Spawning barbel were observed on 56 occasions. A ripe female swims up to the gravel shallow followed by a group of up to six smaller males. Sometimes one or more of the males was chased away by a male upstream of it. The female then nestles on a gravel patch, surrounded by the males which vie for position by her flanks, she then rapidly flaps her tail to dislodge gravel, digging a hole and releasing her eggs which are fertilised by the males. The sticky eggs attach to the newly cleaned gravel to begin their incubation of around 10-15 days, nestling below the surface of the disturbed river bed. This deliberate disturbance of the gravel may be important both to hide the eggs and to de-silt the area allowing a better oxygen supply to the developing larvae. The female leaves the spawning area soon after releasing her eggs, accompanied by the small group of jostling males - perhaps the males are establishing dominance during this phase so that it is clear (to them) which ones will accompany the next ripe female to arrive at the spawning site.

When more than 5 males accompanied a ripe female the spawning attempt was usually unsuccessful because of too much 'sparring' between males. Perhaps the female gives up because the newly-released and vulnerable eggs would be disturbed too much or perhaps because so much conspicuous fighting could make the whole group vulnerable to predation in the shallow water. Even spawning barbel retain their wariness. Whatever the real biological reasons, most successful spawning attempts occurred when only two or three males accompanied a ripe female barbel.

Not many people get the chance to observe fish so closely - it must be fascinating to gain these insights into fish behaviour in the wild. The Driffield Beck barbel know their habitat intimately, distributing themselves over a long length of river with eggs, fry and juveniles living in the shallow streamy headwaters and, for most of the year, adults in the deeper downstream sections. This shows the importance of maintaining migration routes for fish in river systems and of the key importance of the availability of different types of habitat at various stages of the fish's life cycle.

On the River Ourthe, a tributary of the R. Meuse in southern Belgium Etienne Baras also studied barbel spawning behaviour but during very hot weather and under low-flow conditions in 1993. On the Meuse, barbel sometimes spawned at night, especially when there were large temperature fluctuations during the day. Maybe this occurs sometimes in Britain during unusually hot summers. Baras also often observed successful spawnings where a female barbel was accompanied by between 8 and 37 males. So, in the River Ourthe, where there are very few remaining spawning shallows, the reproductive behaviour of the barbel is modified to accept inevitable over-crowding.

Barbel and the weather

© Clare Yates

Water warmth is felt by the whole body of a fish, the temperature of its environment affecting its every behaviour. Feeding activity is particularly temperature-sensitive because the rate at which a fish's metabolism runs is governed directly by body temperature which, in turn, is governed by the surrounding water. Some continuously-swimming sea fish such as tuna may often maintain higher muscle temperatures than the surrounding sea water and so are warm-blooded to a degree but barbel are nowhere near active enough to do this and are effectively controlled by their watery environment.

Etienne Baras has found when radio-tracking barbel that fish may be active from zero to 6 hours per day at different times of year, depending upon the water temperature. During the autumn cooling of rivers, when water temperatures are around 9-10 degrees C barbel are often active for periods during the day as well as at the typical summer dawn and dusk times. As the water cools further the nocturnal, then twilight, then daytime activity bursts progressively vanish until, at around 4-4.5 degrees C, most barbel activity stops. Baras believes that barbel choose to be most active when water temperatures are ideal for them to digest their food.

Warm water-loving fish like barbel are able to detect and respond to tiny temperature changes of a fraction of a degree Celsius. It is crucial to understand that these fish are phenomenally sensitive to changes in temperature; a cold snap can kill off all prospects of winter sport for the carp or barbel angler, whilst an influx of 'warm' rain can turn on the feeding of previously lethargic fish. In summer, warm thundery weather with frequent heavy showers and a warm breeze can make carp, tench and barbel feed like there is no tomorrow, eels (unfortunately!) also respond well to these conditions. Cool water-adapted salmon and trout are, of course, usually affected oppositely. Many fish can probably sense changes in the weather in advance, so well tuned-in are they to prevailing conditions. In this way, sea trout, for instance, will start to run upstream in advance of a band of rain, meeting the rising waters as the spate develops, helping them make best progress towards their headwater spawning streams.

Maybe barbel prepare to feed as they feel weather and light conditions adjusting to their liking, keeping a 'weather eye' open. Stuart Morgan and others believe that it is possible to predict just when barbel are likely to be catchable from weather forecasts (see below). The tendency to feed is governed fundamentally by water temperature and, in particular, whether the temperature has reached critical levels and is rising or falling over a period of days. The following 'rules of thumb', discovered over many years of observation by keen barbel anglers, are traditionally thought to form a reasonable guide for success:

Temperatures below 4 degrees C, especially in frosty, clear-water conditions, or low and falling temperatures due to the influx of snow-melt or reservoir release water indicate minimal feeding activity and difficult fishing.

Temperatures of more than 7 degrees C and especially if the water temperature is rising, eg after warm rain and with coloured water, indicates active feeding and the likelihood of a wet landing net. Water the colour of medium-strong tea is good for barbel fishing and clear 'bottle' green for winter chub and roach fishing.

The best fishing weather for many species is produced by a steady warm, wet, overcast south-westerly air stream. Remember the old poem:

*When the wind is in the north, the fishes don't come forth,
When the wind is in the east, the fishes bite the least,
When the wind is in the south it blows the bait into their mouth and
When the wind is in the west, the fishes bite the best.*

However, as with most animal behaviour, there are subtle variations on these themes. Chippenham angler Stuart Morgan who often fishes with Guy Robb has studied weather patterns (from Royal Observatory and Met. Office reports) in relation to barbel angling success on the Great Ouse, Thames and Bristol Avon. Detailed fishing diaries have allowed a careful analysis with some valuable findings. Stuart catches enough big barbel to amply prove his point. He revealed in Angling Times (March 22nd 2000) that fish feeding patterns seem to be linked to air pressure and temperature regimes. If conditions had remained stable for three to four days or more then any marked change would be likely to trigger a feeding spell. The actual levels of temperature and pressure do not seem as important as the sudden change. Interestingly, even a sudden fall in temperature could give rise to good catches, when a stable low pressure system gave way to a high.

Also, moon phases appear important; any change in the weather co-inciding with a new moon (that is, a relatively dark night) is likely to trigger very active feeding. These active feeding spells may last only a few hours so Stuart's advice is to learn to recognise good conditions and to go fishing if you possibly can when the time is right. It's worth explaining this to your boss at work and to your wife.........

Using these principles Stuart encouraged Guy Robb to go barbelling on the evening of Monday March 6th 2000; a stable weather regime changed to a rise in air pressure co-inciding with a new moon - the result was his record barbel. Not bad advice! Stuart has found that river carp respond in similar ways to barbel.

Fish location and the right bait in the right place are added essential ingredients for success; again, hours of observation on the river bank are the best way to learn. Three times Drennan Cup winner (1998, 2000 & 2001), Terry Lampard who has a superb string of big Hampshire Avon and Dorset Stour barbel to his name swears by clear water summer sessions to search out fish locations and features. These are followed by winter sessions in carefully selected swims, timed to coincide with the right weather. Despite what he modestly says, there isn't much luck involved when Terry catches his many specimen fish.

Angler's 6th sense ?

It may well be that anglers with a 'sixth sense' who believe that they 'know' when they are going to catch a big fish have actually tuned in perfectly to weather conditions and how these affect fish behaviour. Years of experience, patient observation and, above all, the knowse to make the critical links lead to success. Such observant anglers are rare - we can all learn from their insights. The reading list at the end of this book is a good place to start.

Clearly, temperature is not everything; light levels and, perhaps, atmospheric pressure also influence fish behaviour. Many, if not most species feed most actively at dusk, presumably when they feel safe and when many invertebrates become more active and venture up onto the surface of stones to graze algae, many drifting away on the current. This late evening feast of 'invertebrate drift' is well known to river-dwelling fish and may be part of the reason why barbel show such a marked natural bout of feeding each day at dusk - both winter and summer.

The barbel's year

January / February

If cold and bleak lethargic barbel may well be tightly shoaled up in slacks or under banks or log-jams. Feeding will be very limited, probably with a small excursion around dusk. Young fish will be sheltering from the current; in gentle side streams, along slack edges or amongst a broken bouldery bed or old bulrush stands. In milder weather, dusk feeding will be more prolonged.

March / April

If mild the tail end of the season can be very productive for big fish. Large females may be as much as one to two pounds heavier with maturing spawn and in better condition than in early summer. In productive rivers where food is abundant the energy-conscious barbel will have balanced judicious bouts of feeding with avoidance of flood flows. Coloured floods fed by warm westerly winds can see many a late season angler lingering long on the bank for that 'last cast'. It's remarkable how late dusk can seem to be when a tremble on the rod tip must only be a minute or two away.....

May / June

Feeding pretty much tails off prior to and during the annual breeding season. This is when the annual growth check is formed on the scales. The actual timing of spawning will vary with temperatures and flows. The chosen breeding place may be only just up- or downstream of the normal summer/autumn home range if habitat quality is good enough. Where historic damage has ruined or removed nearby gravel shallows barbel may be forced to travel many miles upstream or up a convenient side stream. I think it is likely that barbel home to spawn in the general area where they were born - this is what salmonids seem to do and it would make sense for river cyprinids to do similar things. In an environment where good quality habitat is patchy, going back to breed where you survived as a youngster seems like a good evolutionary strategy.

July / August

After spawning, shoaled up barbel linger for a while over gravel bars ' cleaning up' - I'm not sure what this term really means but I guess it's something to do with regaining condition after the rigours of spawning. The newly hatched fry will need warm sheltered conditions if they are to do well. At this time gravel-bedded glides with bulrush and or crowfoot beds are likely to harbour big adult barbel shoals. It is best to avoid fishing close to spawning areas - give the fish a chance to recover and spread back out into their summer feeding areas. Once barbel have moved back into their normal home ranges, stalking them with a free-lined bait trundled through the weed beds is a deadly method in the right hands. Polaroid glasses plus keen eyes may give you the heart-stopping experience of watching a big fish inspect and then take (or, all too often, reject) your bait. The early bird catches the barbel at this time. Be prepared to walk a fair way from the car park, travel light and cover many swims until you happen across some feeding fish. Trotting deep with a centre pin is a likely method in the right glidey swim. Alternatively, trundle a lightly legered bait along with the current, covering likely lies as you go.

September / October

Reckoned by many to be around the best times for barbel, especially in cool summers and in northern rivers. Indian summers can delay peak autumn fishing into November, especially in the south of England or in continental Europe. The barbel are now at their summer best - well fed with abundant weed cover for safety and thronging invertebrate populations to graze from the shallows in the late evening. Through the summer and into the early autumn growth in length is in full swing and a pre-baiting campaign along remote, under-fished stretches can produce some great fish. A good time to touch leger, either upstream or down, depending on the type of swim you are covering. Low flows can still allow free-lining, it's a brilliant way of trundling a large bait back downstream towards you as you slowly regain line, just keeping in touch with the business end of the tackle. Watch out for the fireworks of a confident take and totally unfettered battle.

November / December

November can be as superb as it can be disappointing. I remember fishing the Severals at Ringwood on the Avon one November 5th evening - it was bitterly cold and even the eels left the Bacon Grill alone. The following year, on the same date, the evening was balmy and just as dusk descended a nice medium-sized barbel raced off with my bait. At around the same time, just up the bank a visiting angler got into a ten pounder on a vintage B.James cane Avon rod and 5lb line. I've never seen a bamboo rod bend so far over, eventually to return to needle straightness after the fish was netted. You can't beat a good cane rod for light water barbelling, there is something very nice about battling a strong fish on a handcrafted piece of bamboo. Carbon is king, it seems to me, when heavy weed, snags or heavy water dictate the need for its clinical efficiency. When conditions are gentler, out comes the split cane for that added enjoyment.

We have just taken a quick stroll through some basic barbel biology. Throughout the year your fishery must provide the right habitats for fish to thrive in. The next chapter examines what these habitat requirements are and whether our rivers are providing them.

© Clare Yates

CHAPTER

3

River habitats

© MGN Ltd

Health-checking your fishery for pollution

The protection of water quality in the UK has a long and honourable history; King Richard II in 1388 put in place a regulation forbidding the dumping of animal remains in rivers, the penalty was death! Nowadays, the Environment Agency tend to go for fines - it's more socially acceptable. If you need help in pursuing polluters, try the ACA for advice. Next time you go fishing, have a good look at the river - try to assess how good the water quality really is. The following sections will help you to do this.

Clean water is crystal-clear and odourless; the stream bed will often be silt-free and sparkling, with little blanketing algal growth and, perhaps, lush *Ranunculus* beds wafting in the current. Pollution makes waters cloudy, with an earthy smell; the stream bed will show growths of brown or green films of algae and bacteria and increasing growth of all pollution-tolerant plants. Thick filamentous algae clogging the river bed is a sign of polluted water. Silted gravels with low dissolved oxygen concentrations are common. When nutrient concentrations become too high delicate plant and animal species decline and may disappear whilst a few hardy ones can take over, dominating the river bed. In the worst instances of organic pollution foam will float on a putrid smelling stream which has a stinking mud bed and supports only sewage fungus. Not so long ago streams like this were, sadly, commonplace. We are lucky to live in times when river water quality is improving - past and continuing regulation of industry by the NRA and Environment Agency has delivered many of these benefits.

When assessing a river, as well as using your eyes and nose, you can gauge the quality of water in your fishery quite accurately by poking around with a fine-meshed pond or landing net and looking carefully at the invertebrate animals which are able to live there. These animals have to survive the prevailing conditions the whole year-round and provide an excellent quick indicator of water quality. Where a single water chemistry sample may well miss a short-lived pollution, the invertebrates living in the river are unable to avoid it. Because their populations can take months or years to recover, the number of differing species and their abundance will reflect the recent 'pollution history' of the fishery. If you examine the invertebrates living in a river just above and just below a source of organic pollution such as a Sewage Treatment Works outflow, a big fish farm or a dirty farm yard or food processing plant, you may well see the following pattern:

In the cleaner water upstream you could find shrimps, cased caddis flies, mayfly nymphs and river limpets. Where the polluting waters enter the river you might only find rat-tailed maggots, bloodworms, tubifex worms and, in bad cases, 'sewage fungus'. As the river dilutes the pollution and recovers downstream, the following invertebrates would start to re-appear; hog lice, wandering snails, alderfly larvae and leeches. In cleaner water still; blue-winged olive nymphs, some caseless caddis larvae, blackflies and blanket weed and finally shrimps, stoneflies varied caddis larvae and *Ephemera* mayfly nymphs. This distribution of animals doesn't happen by accident, the presence of the different species is governed by the quality of the water.

It is well worth getting to know the main groups of freshwater invertebrates; the knowledge will re-pay the learning many times over. In simple terms, if you have plenty of shrimps, varied caddis larvae and mayfly nymphs, then throw your fishing hat in the air, if you've got only hoglice, a leech or two, bloodworm and tiny tubifex worms, things aren't so rosy.

The book by John Goddard (Waterside Guide) will help you to identify what you find in your net samples. Wash them free of silt and empty them into a white enamel or plastic tray. Look at the smaller species with the aid of a hand lens to help with identification. The bigger ones are easily observed with the naked eye. Remember, too, that the bigger juicier species such as alder fly and caddis fly larvae are worth trying as baits. As barbel grow up on a diet of invertebrates and as few anglers bother to collect them for bait, a return to nature may well yield some surprisingly good results. Don't, however, use crayfish or lamprey larvae - it used to be OK but you could, rightly, be lynched these days for breaking conservation laws or local fisheries byelaws.

On March 6th 1960, at Ibsley Bridge on the Hampshire Avon, Charles Cassey was spinning for spring salmon for which the river was very famous when he foul-hooked an immense barbel. The fish was landed, weighed at 16lb 1oz by Colonel Crow, the river keeper and, subsequently, sent to the taxidermist. Who would contemplate doing that now? The stomach was packed with alder fly (*Sialis*) larvae - insects which live in silty river beds. That huge barbel had been feeding actively in late winter by painstakingly sorting sediments along the margins of the Avon for individual invertebrates when a slowly-spun prawn - another natural bait - led to its demise.

Alder fly larvae are pretty big and succulent when full-grown (maybe 3cm long) compared with most aquatic insects but they are still seemingly 'small beer' for such a big fish. Don't be fooled - even the biggest of barbel is partial to a natural bait, especially one which they don't associate with the danger of being caught. Imagine catching a 16lb barbel on a fly larva (other than a maggot)......come to think of it, imagine catching one that big by any method! I speak as someone with a personal best fish of 12lbs 2oz.

What invertebrates can you expect to find in your barbel rivers? Much depends upon the chemistry of the water. The following section should help.

In fast upland river sections, such as the upper Welsh Dee or Rivers Severn, Swale or Wye, mayfly and stone fly nymphs and black fly and caddis larvae which cling to rock surfaces or crawl through moss dominate the invertebrate community. On slower rivers like the Bristol Avon, Lower Trent or Great Ouse animals which can only tolerate slower currents are better able to survive and gravel and silt beds harbour myriads of midge and alder fly larvae, shrimps, caddis larvae, snails, mussels, burrowing mayfly nymphs, lamprey larvae, crayfish and minnows. Chalk and limestone rivers have these groups too but in even greater abundance.

Clean barbel rivers support a vast array of invertebrate food for fish; each square metre of clean gravel can support many thousands of invertebrates - many of them very small. Bank side fringing vegetation where barbel sometimes forage under cover of darkness often harbours many larger species of insect nymphs and other invertebrates. Where bank side fringes are cut back or dredged out invertebrate communities and fish suffer badly.

Careful observations of barbel behaviour on your fishery will help you understand where their main feeding areas are and how you may manage to capture your local specimen fish on natural baits. Barbel feed hardest from June to September - this is when most invertebrates are themselves growing most quickly and when obvious barbel growth in length occurs on the scales. Annual growth in length slows towards November after which it tails off to virtually zero but, as mentioned elsewhere, barbel fatten and mature eggs in winter. Quality home-grown barbel come from clean rivers with good quality habitat and thriving invertebrate populations.

Barbel in polluted waters

In 1993 C.R.Tyler and S.Everett of the Barbel Study Group and Brunel University published a very interesting study of body abnormalities in barbel from the Rivers Teme, Kennet and Lee. The water quality in the sandstone-fed Teme was classified as 1A, in the suburban chalk stream River Kennet it was poorer at 1B and in the obviously polluted urban River Lee with its extensive treated sewage inputs it was class 2. The River Lee catchment had a human population of around 2 million people - the 11,000 cubic metres of treated sewage effluent entering the river daily in 1994 represented 80% of the river flow in dry periods....ughh.

In the 17th Century Izaak Walton described the Lee as amongst the best and most diverse coarse fisheries in the south of England ....what would the amiable old buffer think of it now ?

All barbel examined, about a hundred from each river, were caught by six anglers during the course of a single fishing season. The following problems were recorded if present on captured fish : tumours, ulcers, eye problems, red skin patches, extra barbules, fin damage and mouth sores caused by hook damage. It's well worth having a look at your own barbel to check for these conditions- this can often be done in the water, without the need for netting and landing fish.

In my experience it is rare to spot health problems on barbel, but, I must remember, that I normally fish the Hampshire Avon, Dorset Stour, upper Bristol Avon and middle Wye - rivers with generally good water quality and healthy fish. I've been lucky enough to catch double figure fish from all of these rivers and they have all been in immaculate condition. Having said that, it's not unknown for Avon and Stour barbel to have tumours and extra barbules so perhaps my spectacles are slightly rose-tinted.

Key results of the Brunel University pollution study were:

- On the clean-watered Teme 3% of barbel examined had extra barbules, 2% eye problems and none had skin tumours.
- On the Kennet, with its 'good' water quality, 7% had extra barbules, 10% eye problems and 2% skin tumours.
- On the Lee, with its 'poor' water quality, 34% had extra barbules, 72% eye problems and 25% skin tumours.

It appears that, as water quality deteriorates, obvious abnormalities and health problems in barbel increase markedly. Barbel of all sizes seemed equally likely to have problems and individual fish with health problems were likely to have more than one condition. As well as extra barbules, eye problems and skin tumours, R. Lee barbel also had more ulcers, red skin patches, split fins and mouth hook damage than fish from the other two rivers. It is possible that the 36% of R.Lee barbel with bleeding skin patches on their bellies were directly affected by chemical pollutants in the sediments of the river bed. It is a tribute to the sturdiness of barbel that, despite the problems, the River Lee population still supports very popular and well known fisheries.

The study does not prove that dirty water caused the problems (other factors, such as angling pressure could be involved) but the association is likely to be causal. It's not rocket science; dirty water equals sick fish. Good water quality, along with adequate flows and good river structure (shallows and pools) are the key to good quality coarse and game fisheries.

By keeping an eye on the health of fish you catch, the condition of the water and river bed and the sorts of invertebrates which live in your river you can gain an lot of information on the quality of your fishery. Improved understanding also adds enjoyment to fishing. If you are concerned, have a chat with your Area Environment Agency staff to check out what information they have on your river and what plans are in hand to improve it. Partnership projects, sharing funding and expertise can often work out well. Employing a specialist fisheries consultant to put together a well-targeted management plan for your fishery is also well worth considering.

Pollution is still killing barbel

In summer 2000 the lower Welsh Dee was hit by a catastrophic pollution after heavy rain - thousands of fish were wiped out including many specimen chub and barbel. Some of the biggest fish were probably over twenty years old - how can a quality stock like that be replaced? As I write, the cause of the pollution remains unknown. Maybe it was a slug of de-oxygenated water moving through after a storm washed organically-rich water and sediments out of side ditches or, perhaps, someone threw some nasty chemicals around and got away with it. Water pollution can have devastating long-term effects. Even with restocking, it can take many years for the coarse fishery to return to anything like its former quality. I hope the ACA get to the bottom of the problem and bring any offenders to book.

This is a salutary reminder that your river fishery is never safe, wherever you live. Keep an eye open for fish in distress - there may still be time to do something about it if you act quickly. The Environment Agency has an emergency freephone number 0800 807060 (it's on your rod licence). Take a note of it and use it to alert the EA of problems on your fishery - that's partly what the staff are there for.

Habitats : how do rivers work ?

© Clare Yates

River habitats include the chemical environment of the fish, the levels of flow through the year, the physical structure of the river channel and surrounding land use influencing the catchment.

Water is heavy, viscous stuff. Water currents are generated by the pull of gravity and counterbalanced by the friction of the banks and stream bed. A barbel hugging a boulder-strewn river bed or next to some tree roots lives in an area where the current is slowed by friction. If the fish moves out to catch a drifting worm it has to battle against higher current speeds and will be displaced downstream. Currents are generally fastest in mid-stream and close to the surface - most fish avoid these areas.

Changes in agricultural patterns in recent years have led to the ploughing up of extensive grassland riparian meadows to be replaced with potato, maize and cereal fields. Soil erosion from many of these ploughed fields has been severe and sediment inputs to adjacent rivers have been very high. Extensive field drainage speeds the shedding of water from the land. Where currents are rapid and turbulent, sediment is swept downstream, when current speeds fall (eg close to the bed) sediment settles out, densest particles first. This clogs river beds, filling in the spaces between gravel, killing invertebrates, plants and suffocating fish eggs - bad news for fisheries. High volumes of sediment also fill in river channels and can block sluices and weirs - bad news for people living in properties vulnerable to flooding. Land use seriously affects river habitat quality.

Many upland 'spate' rivers run over impervious rocks such as granite or basalt, these systems are often of steep gradient and respond to prolonged rain by sudden flooding. River levels will rise suddenly and then rapidly drop back to normal. Summer low-flows can leave the bulk of the channel high and dry with only rivulets joining sequences of shallow pools and bank undercuts. Many upland streams have avoided the worst of the siltation impacts experienced downstream as they have fewer arable areas and are better flushed-out by spates.

Clay-bedded rivers are typical of many lowland vales, they tend naturally to behave more placidly with less peaky spates and more sustained summer flows. Extensive agricultural drainage has, however, changed this pattern on many lowland rivers, speeding run-off and increasing the intensity and frequency of floods. Marginal marshes and bogs which used to absorb rainfall, releasing it slowly to sustain flows during droughts are now a rarity. Of course this means that where wetlands have been drained to 'improve' marginal agricultural land, even lowland rivers tend to become more 'spatey' with rapid flood flow responses and lower summer levels. Unfortunately, this has happened on a wide scale in the UK. Most British lowland rivers have been grossly modified through dredging, re-alignment, water abstraction and had their marginal wetlands drained for intensive agriculture. Their fisheries and conservation values have fallen drastically as a consequence.

Furthermore, water quality has been widely affected through the influence of intensive livestock or arable farming along river valleys. As noted above, where old pasture has been ploughed close to rivers or where livestock trample banks, soil inputs have often increased hugely, blanketing the bed with choking silt. This may be the most serious factor affecting river fishery quality in many areas, especially for fish like barbel, chub, trout, salmon and lampreys which must spawn on clean gravel shallows. Less obvious but widespread fisheries impacts from intensive farming are caused by polluting pesticides such as synthetic pyrethroid (SP) sheep dip which can wipe out invertebrate life for hundreds of metres or several kilometres, depending on the severity of the pollution. Herbicide use is also commonplace and fertilisers, silage liquor, cattle or pig slurry, milk and food processing products all often find their way into rural rivers, polluting them badly.

Organically-rich effluents soak up virtually all of the dissolved oxygen, snuffing out all life. Intensive agriculture is bad for river valleys, the quality of fisheries and wildlife communities has declined as a consequence. This is a hidden environmental cost of 'cheap' food production. Sustainable farming is essential for the future well-being of people and wildlife alike.

Urban rivers face industrial pollution of many kinds as well as large volumes of treated sewage effluent and run-off from roads, etc. Sewage effluent contains a range of chemical compounds which have recently been shown to affect the sexual maturity of coarse fish, changing male roach to females, for instance. The degree of damage done to fisheries through this gender-bending remains unclear at present. Once again, more research required. Rivers face a polluting onslaught from all sides, think yourself lucky if you fish a relatively clean one. All of these sources of pollution erode the quality of river habitats and their ability to support sustainable fisheries.

In chalk stream areas it is quite common for streams to lose water through some stretches of river bed and to have active springs rising through the bed in others. Flows can, therefore, fluctuate to some extent as you go downstream. Flow depletion can also occur adjacent to bore holes and downstream of where large scale abstractions are taking place. Over-abstraction seriously damages the ecology of all types of river and many catchments currently have abstraction licences in place which could virtually dry up the river if used to their full extent. The true environmental value of water is not appreciated by the public. Water wasted washing the car or watering the lawn is no longer available to wetland wildlife. What a great excuse for not washing the car - dirty cars can mean more kingfishers!

Barbel habitat production

At the upland end of a catchment, where there tends to be a relatively steep gradient, the river has a high energy, complex, turbulent flow. As the water flows downhill it dissipates its energy, eroding banks as it does so and picking up sediment which it starts to transport downstream. The friction with the stream bed produces upward eddies and currents which we call turbulence. The turbulent currents provide the lift to 'pick up' sediment particles and suspend them in the water column as they are carried downstream. The friction of the water on the stream bed also rolls particles along by subjecting them to 'shear stress'; through this process streams grade sediment particles, sorting them into size classes which decrease with a slowing current and increase with an increasing one. Sorted gravels are an important natural spawning habitat for salmon, trout, grayling, dace, chub and barbel, as well as bullheads and lampreys. Clean, relatively silt-free gravel lies at the heart of a sound river fishery.

In the fastest sections only boulders will stay put on the stream bed, all other sediments are swept away. Even in these torrential upper reaches, however, the rough stream bed and banks slow the flow so that there is a layer of slacker water hugging the bottom. Fish and invertebrates can shelter from the main force of the current by lying close to the bed and making maximum use of the cover provided by rocks and by the banks. Each boulder resists the current and creates a 'cushion' of slack water in front of it and a sheltered patch of 'dead water' behind. Above this slower layer the flow is turbulent with current speed increasing to reach a peak at the surface and towards midstream. Young salmon and trout thrive in the complex turbulent flows of rocky riffle sections. Typically, an upland stream creates a series of fast riffles and pools, each pool ending in a lip where the water rushes once more down the next riffle. The stream thus creates a series of steps, an aquatic stairway, down the hill. In its upper reaches the stream fish community may be dominated by salmonids, lower down the coarse species start to get a fin-hold on the habitat.

Where do gravel shallows (riffles) and corner pools come from?

As the gradient of the typical stream lessens, progressing down the valley, the coarser sediments are deposited wherever the current speed drops, either as gravel shoals in midstream or on the inside of bends. These inner bend deposits tend to push the water harder into the far bank causing lateral flows which start further erosion and under-cutting. In this way corner pools are formed and the stream starts to meander, cutting banks where the current is strongest and depositing sediments wherever the current slows. Hard banks of rock or clay produce narrower river channels with deeper pools than rivers running through softer sandy or silty soils which are wider and shallower.

Meander sequences are determined when the river is running full bore, bank high, with maximum erosive power. Streams and rivers of all sizes tend to have the same sinuous pattern when viewed from above (or on a map). In fact, meanders tend to be seven to ten river widths apart or eleven to sixteen widths apart if you measure the distance along the stream bed.

As a river flows around a bend the current tends to corkscrew, deepening the eroding bank side and carrying sediment back in a series of return currents across the bed to the slacker water of the inner bend. Silt and mud will settle out at average current speeds of 20 cm per second or below whilst sand deposits at around 20-40 cm per second. When weeds grow in this sediment they trap more silt and narrow the channel, this, in turn, increases the current speed, biting once more into the outside bank of the bend. In this way, over many years, rivers wriggle around their valley bottoms, sometimes cutting through the neck of wide loops to leave an oxbow lake. In meandering sections glides appear between the riffles and pools so as to establish the classic riffle-glide-pool sequence which is characteristic of many natural water courses. Go barbel fishing on the Wye upstream of Hereford or on the Teme upstream of Worcester to see very nice sequences of pools, riffles, runs, and glides with excellent bank side cover from willow and alder trees. Nice barbel habitat.

Freshwater fish are adapted to use these habitats through their life cycle. Riffles, with their fast (jogging pace), broken water, harbour rich populations of caddis larvae, shrimps, mayfly and stone fly nymphs which sometimes lose a foothold and drift away downstream. Fish sheltering behind rocks dart out to take this food as it is swept by on the current. Barbel, chub, dace and salmonids spawn here. Coarse fish fry are swept downstream to end up in slack water along vegetated river edges whilst salmon and trout fry are better able to withstand fast currents although they, too, must use slacker water between rocks until they gain strength. Good habitat provides ample cover for young fish of all species.

Runs are rather slower (quick walking pace) with less turbulence and little or no broken water; the bed is often gravel and well-weeded with crowfoot (*Ranunculus*). Adult and maturing grayling, larger trout, barbel, dace and chub occupy such habitat, especially where overhead cover is afforded by bank side vegetation or stands of bulrush or crowfoot. Sections of the Hampshire Avon or Kennet spring to mind.

Flats or glides (strolling pace) have beds of sand or fine gravel and grade into the final category of pools where slack water provides a resting place for species such as roach, bream, perch, pike and eels. Many pools with fast water at their head are used as refuges by specimen barbel, chub and trout which have learnt to exploit the shelter which they provide, venturing out at night to go hunting for food. I know a weir on the upper Bristol Avon where you can lie on your stomach close by the upstream lip of the pool and watch small shoals of barbel cruise past in the clear water only a metre or two away- it's magic.

In any river habitat, different fish species have to balance their key biological needs for comfort (oxygen, temperature, current speed, light level), safety and food supply. Each species of fish has its own preferred combination of these factors and individual fish compete to position themselves to gain the best lies. Successful fishermen learn to 'read the water' and are able to predict where the best lies, holding the biggest fish, will be. This sort of ability adds to the sixth sense which some anglers use to great effect.

Fish habitat zones in rivers

The famous fish biologist Marcel Huet noted that the gradient of a river bed and the current speed are of fundamental importance for the types of fish which usually inhabit a given stretch of river. An adult barbel, for instance, can swim at around 440 cm per second whilst a mature bream can only manage 60 cm per second, going at full steam. The physical challenge of battling the flow is a fundamental factor in river fish distribution. Huet proposed a system of classifying European river zones by the dominant fish species present :

Torrential zone : for instance, the uppermost mountain headwaters of many salmon rivers.

Current speeds here peak at 90-120 cm/sec, the bed is rocky or with heavy cobbles and the water cold. No fish live here, conditions are too fierce and only a few well-adapted plants and invertebrates withstand the environmental conditions.

Trout zone : for instance, the Rivers Dart, Teign, Usk, upper Wye, Severn headwaters, Teifi, Eden. Current speeds cover a range of 30-90 cm/sec but with many sheltered lies. The bed is clean shingle grading to gravel and the water cool and well oxygenated. The gravels are sorted by the river to occur in bands of even size, providing vital spawning habitat freely percolated by well-oxygenated water where eggs incubate for many weeks each winter.

© MGN Ltd

The fish community of the trout zone is dominated by salmonids; salmon parr, trout of all ages, plus minnows, bullheads, stone loach and, in silted corners, eels and the larvae of lampreys. Less harsh stretches may harbour dace and barbel. Mosses and algae coat stable rocks giving shelter to stone fly and mayfly nymphs, caddis larvae, shrimps and freshwater limpets. These, together with beetles, caterpillars, worms, grasshoppers, flying ants, etc falling onto the water from bank side vegetation form the staple diet of the fish. Barbel in these rain-fed spatey types of river will be lean and fit. The invertebrate food supply will not be as abundant as on more lowland river types and it may generally be easier to catch fish as they will often be hungry. Average sizes of barbel will, however, tend to be on the low side as egg survival on clean gravels should be high, with many small fish surviving and competing for food.

Grayling zone : for instance, the Rivers Welsh Dee, middle Wye & upper Severn, upper Kennet, upper Hampshire Avon, Dorset Frome. Current speeds are around 20-30 cm/sec, gravel and sand form the typical stream bed, water crowfoot beds dominate riffles and starwort and cress beds dominate glides. Arrowhead, water parsnip and several other plant species are common in silty margins. Water tends to be fairly cool in most summers, dissolved oxygen concentrations remain high and the fish community is dominated by grayling, trout, dace, chub, barbel and eels. Pike and roach live mainly in slacks and backwaters. Invertebrate populations are prolific with huge numbers of black fly and midge larvae, mayfly nymphs, caddis larvae, river limpets and other snails, water beetles, water bugs and shrimps. The invertebrate populations on these rivers make for well-conditioned barbel which may be fairly catchable but are not desperate for food. Where gravels are clean large numbers of young barbel can lead to the production of dense shoals and correspondingly greater competition for food. Here ground-baiting can get barbel feeding through the day and large catches can be built up on the float or feeder.

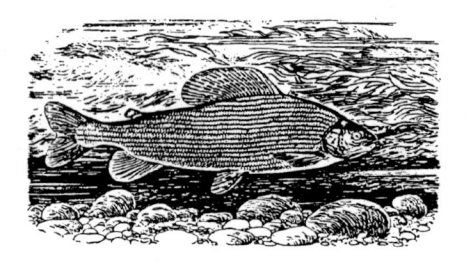

© Clare Yates

Barbel zone : for instance, the Rivers middle & lower Severn , middle Trent, lower Wye, Bristol Avon, upper & middle Great Ouse, lower Wharfe, Warwick Avon, upper Thames, Lee, Windrush, middle and lower Hampshire Avon, middle and lower Dorset Stour. Current speeds are typically around 10-30 cm/sec, features provide sheltered lies and 'creases'. The gravel and sand bed can be moderately silted on the inside of bends, crowfoot dominates fast glides, bulrush beds are common and 'cabbages' (sunken water lilies) occur in slacker glides with marginal reeds, cress, arrowhead and water parsnip. The invertebrate community is similar to the grayling zone on gravel shallows but also includes more silt-dwelling species along pool edges, inner bends and in impounded sections. Temperatures and oxygen concentrations can fluctuate noticeably through the 24 hour cycle and the fish community is usually dominated by barbel, chub, dace, roach, pike, with some bream and sometimes carp in slacker lies. Here, in classic barbel habitat, fish can be fat and choosy, of high average size and not forced to take baits. Silty gravels may, on some rivers, have lead to low numbers of surviving fry and small shoal sizes, competition for food may not, therefore, be intense and here you may find a record-sized fish. Chub can be very abundant and of specimen size in these rivers.

© Clare Yates

Bream zone eg Fenland drains, Rivers lower Thames, lower Great Ouse, lower Nene, lower Trent and lower Bristol Avon. These rivers are classically slow-flowing, meandering lowland sections where conditions can become pond or canal-like in summer. This is especially true on rivers impounded by weirs. Some canals, like the Kennet & Avon provide still water habitats linked to main rivers. Here the water temperatures and concentration of dissolved oxygen fluctuate widely through a summer's day. Oxygen levels may be very low at night in warm weather. On heavily weeded sections respiration by the plants and animals burns up most of the available dissolved oxygen, leaving sensitive species in a delicate state. Fish kills can happen on warm thundery late summer nights, especially if there's a bit of pollution about.

The bream zone is characterised by dense stocks of bream, silver bream, tench, common carp, roach, bleak, gudgeon, perch, pike and eels. Where conditions remain well oxygenated species like barbel, normally found in faster water, will drop back into these zones, especially in winter to avoid violent flows. Large bream shoals can dominate where the sediments are rich enough to support thriving populations of chironomid midge larvae (bloodworms), small mussels and aquatic worms. Lilies, pond weeds, common reed beds, reed sweet grass, reed mace, bur reeds, yellow flag, marsh marigolds, Mare's tail, amphibious bistort and submerged stands of milfoil, Canadian pondweed and broad-leaved pondweeds mingle to provide a wonderful lush green waterscape.

> THIS IS A LIKELY BREAM HOLE, PETER, DEEP AND QUIET AWAY FROM THE HEAVY WATER

> EARLY MORNING OR EVENING IS BEST, THOUGH YOU CAN CATCH BREAM DURING THE DAY

© MGN Ltd

This, then, is the range of natural river habitats within which barbel roam. These fish don't, however, stick just to textbook areas - they select a typical set of conditions which approximates to what we call the 'barbel zone', but can often wander up- or downstream on a whim or whilst on spawning migrations.

River habitat damage

We now know that natural rivers provide :
- Few barriers to migration,
- Clean, abundant water,
- Shallow, relatively silt-free gravelly areas for spawning (riffles),
- Ample physical cover from weed beds, rocks, tree root snags, dead wood and fringing vegetation lying along stream edges,
- Deeper glides with fringing vegetation and corner pools for adult fish to hide in,
- And all intermediate habitats for juvenile and maturing fish to occupy.

As long as your river has a nice varied character - like you would see on the Teme, middle Wye, or upper Severn, for instance, then, other habitat factors (flows, water quality) being adequate, you should expect to find thriving barbel populations.

The problem is that virtually none of our British rivers have remained in good physical condition. Virtually all lowland rivers have been sequentially impounded to provide water power to drive mills, to allow navigation or to increase depths. Dams form barriers to fish migration and upstream silt traps where the current speed is killed and pond-like conditions occur in summer.

Most rivers have been dredged and straightened to varying degrees to increase their flood carrying capacities and to lower summer water tables to help drain wet agricultural land. Gravel shallows have often been taken out completely, the gravel being used to surface tracks or construct roads. Dead wood cover has been stripped out, together with bank side trees, shrubs and fringing vegetation to maximise flood capacity. With a sudden loss of cover many fish are forced to migrate in search of safer havens ….. sadly, they may never find them.

Such things are, however, not new. Patrick Chalmers, in the 1930s reflected sadly on the changes which the Thames Conservancy had instigated at Goring. There, Chalmers had spent hours standing on the old wooden bridge, watching the 'shoals of big barbel pushing and rolling on the golden gravels'. The Conservancy dredgers were brought in to enlarge the weir pool, grubbing out the gravel bar and carting it away. One more piece of barbel habitat gone - once the gravel was removed it couldn't be naturally replaced below the weir. I suppose, on reflection, it is worth noting that the weir pool itself wouldn't have been there without Man's intervention. We affect rivers in many fundamental ways, sometimes for the better and sometimes the worse, fisheries must adapt or perish - it has always been so.

Headwaters of rivers have often been dammed (and damned); flooded to form reservoirs to store winter rainfall and some are used to drive hydro-electric turbines. Over- abstraction of water directly from rivers and lakes and from bedrock aquifers leads to chronic summer low flows with shallow water, siltation of spawning gravels, loss of water crowfoot beds, drying up of spawning side streams and nursery habitats. This sounds quite depressing I realise but hey, all is not lost, river habitats can be improved beyond recognition, sometimes with little money and with excellent fishery results.

In a heavily populated little set of islands like the British Isles it is too much to hope that rivers would have escaped the ravages of development and intensive use of the countryside. The scale of damage imposed has been truly monumental and we are all so used to seeing our rivers the way they are now that many of us have no idea how much better they could be, given some well targeted management and restoration. Chapter 4 gives some examples of successful river habitat restoration projects.

Flood defence and land drainage

A given slope and underlying geology will tend to produce a characteristic river type. Land drainage and flood defence works lower water tables and remove river channel features which retard the flow, fundamentally altering the true character of the river. When rivers have been channelised in this way, removing the natural riffle and pool sequence (and hence most of the good quality fish habitat) but the overall slope remains in the landscape, they will gradually re-create a channel of the original form which will lie deeper down below its banks. Such natural recovery from insensitive past management can be seen in some river sections dredged thirty or forty years ago but, in lowland rivers, the process is slow. Unfortunately, of course, drainage teams may also have returned before then to re-dredge the channel and remove recovering habitat.

The philosophy of deep river dredging for land-drainage and flood defence is, fortunately, now being overtaken by the realisation that more natural river valleys have a number of benefits for society.

These include :

1. Better flood water storage in winter and summer flow support from marginal wetlands which can be re-created along river valleys. This could provide big new wetland areas for wildlife and for people to enjoy for recreation.
2. Better natural water filtering and chemical cleansing in rough grassland buffer zones, reed beds and marshes, all of which can be developed with changed water level management.
3. Better fisheries resources and wildlife conservation which bring recreational opportunities, income and rural employment, often to areas where jobs are desperately needed.

Great, let's get going! As I write this (spring 2002) Government is proposing a modest shift from agricultural subsidies and over-production towards more sustainable farming practices. Let's all hope these changes are implemented soon and on a widespread scale.

Thanks to a growing support for de-intensification of farming along river valleys and some government grant-aid for environmentally sensitive agriculture, some of our wetland wildlife is staging a comeback. Otters in England and Wales are a good example with a sustained spread east from their Celtic fringe strongholds in the west. There is, however, a long, long way to go - many miles of river channel need active restoration schemes. These can be initiated at local levels by angling clubs / riparian owners and on a wider scale by River Trusts, conservation bodies such as The Wildlife Trusts and government agencies such as The Environment Agency, English Nature, Countryside Council for Wales and others.

We can all do our bit to help - the results make the effort very worthwhile - why not get your boots on and get stuck in ? What you need is a fisheries management plan and this must be based on an understanding of the detailed requirements of your target species. Also, it must take account of other wildlife groups - not just fish.

Understanding barbel habitat

© MGN Ltd

Our understanding of fish biology comes largely from scientific studies carried out by trained observers and experimenters. It has become fashionable in some angling quarters to ignore the advice of qualified and experienced ecologists and to assume that perceptions of fisheries problems by riparian owners and anglers are accurate. This is most unwise; many of the sceptics have perfectly reasonable opinions but based largely on conjecture. There is no real substitute for scientific analysis and carefully designed experiments; then, cause and effect can be established. Otherwise, with the best will in the world, the blind can end up leading the foolish. Surely, if scarce resources are to be spent trying to improve fisheries, it must be right to base future work on objective scientific studies which have produced successful results. Sound studies should include un-worked control areas for comparison with experimental stretches. In this way we can discover whether real improvements have actually taken place. Monitoring the outcome of projects is vital and honesty in reporting failures, as well as successes is essential. I return to this topic in the next chapter.

Some ground-breaking research work has been done for barbel and other river coarse fish in Britain and continental Europe but much remains to be done. The overall value of freshwater fisheries to the economy of both urban and rural communities is immense. Kids enjoying themselves on river banks are less likely to embark on a life of crime and more likely to understand and value the environment. Local anglers and holiday-makers also gain enjoyment, spend money on tackle, bait, fuel, accommodation, day tickets, club memberships, etc, etc, generating employment in river valleys. Only river valleys in good environmental shape can support viable wild fisheries.

Habitat for young barbel on the River Lee and other European rivers

Mark Pilcher and Gordon Copp studied the distribution of young coarse fish on Hertfordshire's River Lee in the early 1990s- as we have already seen, the Lee is hard-pressed for water quality but, sadly, the physical habitats have suffered greatly too. Mark and Gordon discovered that young barbel on the Lee only turned up in areas where the channel was narrow, fast-flowing and with a gravelly bed. Barbel breed in the few areas where you still find brown trout. These areas were only found where the river had not been deep-dredged or over-widened by flood defence engineering schemes. Where the river had been dug out, young barbel were absent - simple as that. Young chub and dace showed a similar pattern with only older bigger chub moving into the canalised sections of river. Remarkably, much of the canalisation was carried out in the 18th Century - not that long after Izaak Walton wandered its banks, cane fishing rod in hand - the complete angler. A further batch of dredging projects was carried out in the 1950s. Now, only the upper Lee catchment supports sustainable stocks of fish which need fast-flowing water, the lower river being completely tamed and regulated, a home for perch, pike, bream, tench, eels, plastic bags and super market trolleys.

Gordon Copp and Paul Garner studied the distribution of young coarse fish in the Lee, at Woolmer's Park during the summer of 1995. Amongst their electric fishing catches were barbel of all sizes from fry upwards. When the detailed habitat preferences of young fish of various species were analysed they found that :

- Barbel fry preferred areas close to the bank with overhanging vegetation and where the water was slack. This is also true of the young fry of most coarse fish species.

- One year old and bigger barbel, however, preferred deeper water with a swift current and an open, varied gravel river bed.
- Good barbel nursery habitat on the Lee tends to occur along relatively narrow sections with fringing vegetation, shallow, moderately-flowing with a mixed gravel/pebble bed and abundant (40% or more) cover from bank side trees, shrubs and fringing grasses and reeds.

In other studies of the ecological requirements of coarse fish fry in European rivers, scientists have found that young barbel typically occur where spawning gravels are clean, not silty, where current speeds are slow - 5 to 8 body lengths per second and with plenty of weed cover and where summer temperatures are 15-16 degrees C - pretty warm for rapidly-flowing rivers. Young chub like it even weedier than young barbel do.

Results like these are important - consider what happens to barbel fry habitat if a dredging team removes the vegetation all along the edge of a nursery area or if a summer weed cut suddenly lowers water levels away from the vegetated fringe -disaster! Sheltered fry habitat is wrecked and bigger barbel which use overhanging bank side shrubs and trees for cover are left out in the open. What would happen to your fishery if this vital cover were to be removed?

Tree and shrub clearance effects

Gordon Copp and Tony Bennetts were able to see what happened to the barbel population when the riparian owner suddenly removed about 30% of the bank side trees and 70% of overhanging branches trailing in the water of the River Lee at their study site.

The effects were a significant reduction in the numbers and in the size of resident barbel, especially the largest fish. Presumably, when their preferred habitat was suddenly removed, the bigger barbel were forced to move and search for better cover, a point worth remembering before you get the pruning saw out. This study made me wonder what happened when more extensive 'flood defence' works were carried out during the 1960s, 70s, 80s and beyond.

River dredging effects - the River Soar

Stephen Swales studied the effects of river dredging on the fish populations of the lowland Leicestershire River Soar, a tributary of the Trent. The dredging scheme in late 1978 aimed to reduce flood risk to adjacent farmland (and some houses) and 'improve' soil moisture conditions by dropping normal water table levels to around a metre and a half below bank level. This was achieved over 9.5 kilometres of river by removing gravel shallows, straightening bends (obliterating corner pools) and re-grading banks to widen the channel (ripping out bankside trees and shrubs). By comparing pre- and post-drainage fish surveys, Swales showed that the drainage work reduced the total fish population by about 75%, largely, he thought, through the removal of bank side trees and shrubs which provide vital shelter.

The key results were : brown trout, which were relatively rare before the drainage work started, disappeared from the study stretch altogether, dace numbers fell by 72%, chub numbers fell by 87%. Roach were the most resilient species, with their numbers being reduced by only 30%. Had barbel been present they, too would certainly have suffered.

These effects were likely to be relatively long-lasting for the following reasons :

1. It takes time for trees to re-seed and grow large enough to provide enough cover for sheltering fish shoals.
2. The new uniform river bed channel left by the dredging crew offers little cover or shelter for fish, especially young fish when, in the past, they could shelter behind gravel bars, weed beds, boulders, tree stumps, root masses, etc. Protection from the main current is probably at least as important as cover from predators for the purposes of everyday survival.
3. Gravel spawning bars and corner pools were also taken out....these fundamental habitat features are not likely to recover on their own for many years. Where could the fish spawn now and where could big fish find safe cover?

A key question is - how long do these devastating effects last?

Ian Cowx and colleagues reviewed the state of the River Soar fishery after fish population surveys had been carried out over an 8 year period on the dredged section and on a nearby control area inaccessible to the diggers which remained unaffected by the works.

They found the following key results :

Shortly after the dredging the natural 'control' section, which the dredgers had missed, increased in fish density - probably due to the displacement of fish from the long, badly damaged dredged section. The dredged section remained devoid of fish of interest to anglers for five years until pioneer chub and dace started to move back in, using the small amounts of cover (sparse reed growth) now available in the habitat desert left by the dredging team. The biologists were pretty sure that the sudden, severe change from a nice varied series of gravel shallows and deeper pools with good bank side vegetation cover to a relatively featureless, open, inhospitable gutter had led directly to the fish abandoning their former home. I'm pretty sure they are right.

Just think how often this must have happened when, for instance, over-zealous flood defence programmes stripped river banks clear of virtually all overhanging vegetation and deep-dredged channels. Heavy river engineering and channelisation (very popular in the 1950s, 60s, 70s and 80s) has wrecked huge amounts of formerly excellent fish habitat on our lowland rivers. Anywhere that natural pools and gravel riffles, undercut banks and overhanging trees have been removed to create a uniform over-deep and over-wide channel will be hugely impoverished, both for fish and other river wildlife. Virtually all cover is gone, winter flood flows rip through and low summer flows are spread thinly across the enlarged channel....bad news at all times of year.

Fortunately, the old philosophy is slowly changing and, nowadays, it is less common for serious ecological damage to be done to river channels by flood defence schemes. As a busy fisheries consultant I'm sorry to say, however, that I do still come across it from time to time. Extensive removal of live vegetation, deadwood and sediments (including gravel) is still routine. This ongoing removal of vital cover means that many rivers are still held back from recovering anything like natural fish population densities. The problems are often worst for the fry stages, leading to poor recruitment and the need to stock fish to keep fisheries going. On many rivers these stocked fish may not even get a chance to spawn because of a lack of suitable habitat.

Reversing the damage

On a positive note, just think how much good you can do for barbel habitats on your fishery by replanting trees and shrubs and promoting an abundance of natural fish cover. This will allow your fishery to hold more fish and it will help you to spread out barbel and chub between lots of swims, perhaps getting away from a situation where most fish are holed up in just a couple of well-covered spots which receive too much angling pressure. See the next chapter for some ideas on how to improve your fishery.

Obstructions to barbel migrations

The River Severn and Driffield Beck studies and radio-tracking work on other rivers show how often barbel move over long distances during their normal annual cycle. What happens to barbel stocks on rivers which have series of weirs? How easily can barbel move over these structures?

Martyn Lucas' barbel tracking research on the River Nidd between March and July in 1993 and 1994 followed the movements of 23 barbel which attempted to pass a low (40cm) weir during their attempted spawning migration; only 6 were successful. The weir, built to gauge river flows, was usually approached by fish around dawn or dusk but was only crossed at night. All barbel trying to pass the weir were delayed on their journey. Calculations on the sustained high-speed swimming capabilities of barbel showed that, especially in highly turbulent water where drag effects are high, the fish were probably often exhausted before overcoming the weir crest and reaching slower flows above. Don't forget, this is only a small weir, imagine how difficult it would be for barbel on higher, faster-water weirs. Those fish which eventually made it over the crest of the weir on the Nidd all travelled some distance further upstream to spawn on a series of gravel shallows. Those which failed to cross the weir turned back and moved downstream into areas where gravel shallows are much less common. I wonder whether these barbel found a suitable spawning area or were thwarted and failed to breed ? This situation may be commoner than you think.

Gravel dredging in Belgium - The River Meuse

Studies in Belgium have shed further light on barriers to barbel migration and removal of spawning bars. Between 1989-93 Etiene Baras and colleagues discovered that barbel consistently failed to use a purpose-built Denil fish pass on the River Meuse. This fish pass, designed to by-pass a hydro-electric plant, wasn't managed to maintain an adequate flow of water and so barbel were not attracted to it, preferring instead to shoal at the dead-end entrance to the turbine housings. This meant that no barbel made it upstream to continue their spawning migration in years when the pass had inadequate flows.

River Meuse barbel not only have to try and overcome barriers to migration - they also have to find some gravel to spawn upon. Baras, working in 1993/4 on his Belgian barbel populations of a 10km section of the River Ourthe, a tributary of the River Meuse, developed some horrendous statistics on damage to fish habitats. On this river it has been long term flood defence practice to remove gravel shallows in built-up areas. Over the 10km study stretch Baras could find only six sites, covering less than 900 square metres, where gravel suitable for barbel spawning remained. Electric-fishing surveys showed that these gravel bars were virtually the only areas where young-of-the-year barbel could be found. Any mature barbel trying to spawn would have to find these small areas over 10km of river. To make things worse, dredging works were being contemplated which would have reduced the area of these nursery habitats by a further 98%!

No wonder barbel have to migrate long distances to spawn on some heavily engineered European river systems.

Just think what a difference putting a few well-placed gravel shallows back into such rivers can make. I have done just this for trout and grayling on the upper Bristol Avon and the Wiltshire Wylye and had fish spawning on the new gravels within weeks of putting them in ..... why not help develop similar work for our coarse fish on a widespread basis on engineered lowland rivers ? Examples of success stories for coarse fisheries habitat improvements are given in the next chapter.

A 'blueprint' for the Hampshire Avon ?

> WE'LL DO IT THE WAY THEY DO ON THE HAMPSHIRE AVON — AND THEY GET MAGNIFICENT BARBEL THERE

© MGN Ltd

A few decades ago spring salmon fishing accounted for the bulk of fishery incomes on the lower Avon - the fish averaged over twenty pounds and were readily caught in spring on spinners, plugs and spun natural baits. Now, in common with many salmon rivers, there are hardly any 'springers' left. However, as on the Wye, Hampshire Avon fishery incomes have been underpinned by barbel anglers who have exploited the rise in barbel stocks in these and other rivers as beats have been relinquished by salmon rods and become available to new, less affluent tenants. The quality of the Avon is not what it once was. Poor recruitment of salmon and brown trout is a well-known fact on the river. Now, young barbel are being stocked on some well known fisheries as natural regeneration appears not to be taking place - this needs urgent study if the river is to be managed effectively in the long term. It may be that spawning is successful in just a few good areas of habitat. If this is the case then habitat improvement on a wider scale could help.

Recently, I have been helping two large Avon estates to improve river habitats for game and coarse fish as well as for the wealth of wetland wildlife for which the Avon Valley is famous. Factors thought to need addressing include (in no particular order):

- Historic gravel bar removal and deep-dredging schemes.
- A lack of marginal slow current habitats for fish fry.
- Arable farming too close to river banks, with few buffer zones.
- Pollution inputs from a variety of sources.
- Bank erosion - over-grazing by cattle and a lack of fencing in key areas.
- Chronic siltation of spawning gravels.
- Loss of wet meadows through agricultural drainage and water level management.
- Important spawning side streams which have fallen into disrepair, becoming over-shaded and trampled to oblivion by livestock.
- Barriers to fish migration.

I have recently surveyed wonderful Avon stretches at Breamore and Bisterne and look forward to including other estates in my reports. This is a good example of caring riparian owners acting to develop plans for fishery improvements which can then be implemented as funds become available. Grant-aid from agencies such as English Nature and the Environment Agency are a tremendous help in this respect. It is important to meld fisheries aspirations with more general conservation objectives. I hope that, in years to come, habitat improvement projects will spur-on increases in salmon, wild trout, grayling, dace, chub, roach and barbel stocks as well as producing better habitats for redshank, snipe, lapwings, water crowfoot, water voles, otters, lampreys, bullheads and many other species besides. Really worthwhile and enjoyable work.

This chapter has considered river habitats and some of the problems they face. The next chapter shows that these problems are not insurmountable and that, with a little help from their friends, great improvements in rivers can be generated, often at modest cost.

CHAPTER

4

Fishery management

> THE BARBEL FIGHTS LONG AND HARD

© MGN Ltd

20th - 21st Century barbel fisheries

In 1988, Crowood published the ground-breaking 'Barbel' by the Barbel Catchers (Club) & friends and put together by that well known travelling angler John Bailey. At the time of writing this book (summer 2002), times have changed somewhat; let's revisit the Barbel Catchers 1988 book to appreciate how things were less than 15 years ago:

The historic list of huge Hampshire Avon barbel was dominated by the originator of the cane Avon rod - the wizard of the Royalty, F.W.K. Wallis who caught (amongst many others) fish of 13lb 4oz, 13lb 5oz and 13lb 8oz in 1934, culminating in his record fish of 14lb 6oz in 1937. Wallis was a master barbel fisher but he didn't land the biggest of the Royalty's barbel: in April 1931 Roy Beddington, a salmon angler, had foul-hooked a huge 16lb 8oz fish. Barbel of up to an estimated 20lbs were reported seen but never landed on the fishery. Few anglers believe that the Royalty holds such mega-barbel these days but, you never know!

The Barbel Catcher's Club 1988 all time top 50 fish was topped by a 14lb 2oz fish from either the Hants Avon or Dorset Stour caught by Pete Reading in 1988, closely followed by a 14lb 1oz Stour fish by Greg Buxton in 1985. Four thirteen pounders and eleven twelve pounders propped up these fish - all of these barbel came from the Avon, Stour or Wensum, with just one from the Great Ouse. Whilst musing on the future of barbel fishing from the 1988 perspective, Pete Tillotson made the following points :

The Wye looked a good bet for developing a thriving barbel stock (quite right!) but the signs for the 14lb 6oz record being broken were not regarded as good. Of course, it's easy to be wise with hindsight, but I'm sure that Pete would have been surprised at just how successful anglers have been at winkling out massive barbel in the 1990s, had he had a crystal ball.

Ten years on, Angler's Mail, in November 1998, for instance, noted that to qualify for a top 50 barbel a fish needed to be above 14lb 12oz, with a 15 pounder perhaps becoming the benchmark for a 'specimen' fish. The November 1998 article featured a string of very big fish caught over recent years: in 1992, 14lb 6oz 8dr, 14lb 9oz and14lb 13oz. In 1993 15lb 7oz and 15lb 11oz. In 1994 16lb 2oz. In 1997 16lb 3oz, 16lb 5oz (by Ray Wood, not claimed as record) and in 1998, 16lb 6oz and16lb 11oz. In 1999 bigger barbel still were caught by Martin Bowler (16lb 12oz), Guy Robb (17lb 6oz) and Trevor Wilson (17lb 10oz) - all from the Great Ouse in Bucks. By March 2000 the Great Ouse produced a 17lb 6oz 12dr fish for Guy Robb, a 17lb 7oz for Gareth Hancock, and barbel of 17lb 9oz and 17lb 14oz for Stuart Morgan. January 2001 saw Tony Gibson land a Great Ouse 19lb fish only to be topped in October by Steve Curtin's 19lb 6oz whopper from Adam's Mill. This is the biggest authenticated rod caught barbel at the time of writing this book but we haven't reached the end of the season yet. Many of these latter day Barbus maximuses were lured on state-of-the-art John Baker boilie and paste baits - a big switch from the more traditional approach.

Barbel nosing over the river bed - sensory pads on lips and barbules.

Big strong mouth, sensitive barbules, huge powerful pectoral fins.

Daytime . . . happy, hiding under a log.

Moving out to feed at dusk.

Chris Yates with a late evening Avon beauty.

Spring and early summer - minnows on the menu..

Shoaling - competition for food.

Pete Reading, Dorset Stour 14lb 9oz specimen.

Pete Reading, Great Ouse, 1999 'The Pope' at 15lb 12oz.

Chub often share cover with barbel.

Dace love fast gravel runs at the head of barbel swims.

Edward Barder with his splendid current record Kennet barbel, February 2002. Well-built cane rods can handle very big fish with no problems.

Big roach share steady glides with barbel.

Edward Barder with a readily-recognisable crinkle-finned 15lb 4oz Kennel barbel known to be between 30 and 40 years old, and still going strong!

Flotsam raft - overhead cover for Great Ouse chub and barbel..

Perfect pool habitat, the Great Weir, Royalty Fishery, Hampshire Avon.

Dave Burr, River Wye - an immaculate day time barbel.

Red Lion Hotel

River Wye · Bredwardine · Herefordshire · HR3 6BU

Telephone 01981 500303

Probably the best barbel fishing in the country!

Gently returned to fight another day.

Bristol Avon barbel fry - leviathan of the future?

River Kennet sidestream - nice juvenile barbel habitat.

Upper Bristol Avon. lovely pool and riffle - barbel and chub heaven.

Wrecked river habitat, dredging upper Great Ouse, 1980s.

Restored river habitat, Bristol Avon, downstream of Malmesbury.

Signal crayfish - alien river invader and new food source for chub and barbel.

Standard barbel fare; caddis larvae on the underside of a River Teme boulder.
Clean water = a varied food source.

Ian Watson with lithe 10lb 15oz Wye barbel, Bredwardine.

Cock salmon pre-spawning - do barbel really affect salmon stocks?

Those big droopy barbules are built for sniffing out food.

Hoovering the gravel bed in search of invertebrates.

Clean water, gravelly bed - shrimps, *Gammarus*.

Clean water, silted gravels - mayfly nymphs, *Ephemera*.

Slower water, maybe some enrichment - water louse, *Asellus*.

Slower but clean water - wide range of caddis larvae.

Slack water, weedy areas - snails on the menu.

Silted backwaters and margins - Alder fly larva, *Sialis*.

A classic barbel plus bamboo rod and centre pin reel.

Barbel fishing is fun - Chris Yates and Sue Carter celebrate a middle Avon fish.

In the 1998 Angler's Mail feature Ray Walton rated the likely rivers to produce even bigger barbel in the next ten years to be the Great Ouse, Medway, Severn, Trent, Wensum and Wye, next tier the Bristol Avon, Dove and Thames and then the Hampshire Avon, Kennet and Dorset Stour. He was spot-on with the Great Ouse although it seems likely that not that many fish are involved in the recent record chase going on there. The great thing about the above list is the wide range of river systems which could potentially produce a new record barbel, giving us all a fighting chance of that ultimate 'personal best'.

Could a 20 pound British barbel grace a landing net in the new Millenium? Respected anglers like Dick Walker certainly claimed to have seen barbel estimated to weigh around 20lb in the 1960s on the Hampshire Avon. Fish of that size could be there still. John Ginifer tangled with a barbel on the clear-watered Potts stream, Oxford, a very productive Thames tributary, which he estimated at around 20lb and he had a close look at it, peering over the side of his canoe (John, not the barbel).

Since John's Oxford days the Potts stream, in common with so many Thames tributaries has declined markedly in quality - Barbus maximus probably no longer graces its waters. More recently (July 1985), Chris Yates saw a monster barbel safely tucked away above the chain in a 'no-fishing area' on the lower Avon at the head of the Parlour Pool on the Royalty Fishery. That fish was nearly caught on a number of occasions (see The Deepening Pool) but evaded all attempts and is now presumed to have disappeared to the great barbel swim in the sky.

In addition to the Great Ouse, Avon and Thames, the lower Severn, Trent or Wye could easily be harbouring twenty pound barbel even now and I wouldn't mind betting that a fish of this size will be caught before many more seasons. Very big barbel are so wary that they could evade capture for many years, especially in large rivers where they are unlikely to be seen and where location will tend to be difficult. A concerted campaign in the right location could soon produce a new stamp of UK barbel. With the advent of global warming and its mild, wet winters and hot summers plus a diet of high protein baits, barbel growth rates could well be set to increase markedly in future years.

Outside the UK in warm productive waters *Barbus barbus* grow very large - John Bailey has tipped the Czech Republic, western Russia and Poland where he believes 30 pounders could be a possibility. If mega-barbel really take your fancy you might consider a summer holiday in Spain where *Barbus comizo*, a similar species to our *B. barbus*, grows to at least 35 pounds. This exciting large-finned, hard fighting barbel occurs in rivers and in some lakes above dams; one such water south of Madrid regularly produces twenty pounders which grow fat on a diet including crayfish. Tackle requirements are substantial as these fish fight easily as hard as the carp which also frequent the lake.

In fact, in terms of tactics, these really are a modern carp-fisher's barbel. For example, fishmeal boilies on size 2 hooks, 15lb line and 3lb test curve rods were used by Graham Lawrence, a visiting British angler who shared a 14 fish bag over the course of a week's fishing - all of the barbel weighing over ten pounds. What would Mr Crabtree have made of it all?

For those more traditional barbel fishers among you, consider a Spanish alternative - 'gypsies'. Gypsy barbel look similar to our *Barbus barbus* but these fish have stunning dark mahogany backs and butter yellow / orange bellies. They live mostly in unspoilt rushing southern Spanish rivers with gravel shallows and shimmering pools in the cool of deeply cut valleys and need to be stalked with stealth and watercraft. If you like it hot you can pursue them across desert drainage systems where they lie up in cover during the day, sliding out to feed as dusk falls. A very big gypsy barbel is twenty pounds plus, thirty pounders turn up regularly - wow! John Bailey knows where they live, if you fancy a trip.

Some western European barbel stocks are in dire need of conservation owing to the destruction of many of their natural deep, slow, weedy river habitats, water pollution and the introduction of exotic predator species. Our barbel species, *Barbus barbus* has been classified as threatened or endangered, for instance in southern Belgium. *Barbus comizo* living in Iberia are now scarce in their former strongholds, the Rivers Tajo and Guadiana and very rare in the Guadalquivir. The species is considered vulnerable in terms of long-term survival whilst several other northern Mediterranean barbel species are now threatened with extinction. Angling tourism could help to provide economic support for their conservation, provided that the remaining stocks are not over-pressured.

Fortunately, UK rivers are, in general, improving in chemical quality and much can be done in terms of physical habitat restoration to ensure the successful conservation of our barbel stocks and the other species which share their homes.

Research on improving barbel habitats

Between 1996 and 1999 I had the chance to carry out some river habitat restoration on the upper Bristol Avon just downstream of Malmesbury, Wiltshire. The Somerfords Fishing Association were worried that over-abstraction was leading to lower than normal summer flows and seriously damaging their game and coarse fisheries. Wessex Water Services Ltd. funded experimental work to have a look at the river and see whether habitat improvements could be made to some previously deep-dredged sections where the channel may have been made too large for prevailing conditions. I walked the river with colleagues from The Game Conservancy Trust and designed a restoration scheme. The key idea was to force the river to scour out some new pools by building a long series of sarsen stone current-deflectors. The sarsen stones were naturally weathered rocks left lying around after the last Ice Age - it seemed appropriate to put them back in the river. The objective of the project, which built upon earlier NRA work carried out by Adrian Taylor and colleagues, was to improve damaged habitats for wild brown trout and grayling, both of which had declined on the river in recent years. A wide variety of coarse fish including barbel, chub, roach, dace and perch which still thrive in the river were also likely to benefit from the work.

The deep-dredging land drainage programme carried out some years before by the Water Authority had removed many natural pools and gravel shallows, leaving long stretches of relatively uniform over-deep river channel. The new boulder current deflectors were designed to scour deep holes and to deposit clean gravel shallows at the pool tails - this worked very well and the boulders have stayed put ever since (six years at the time of writing). Vegetation (reeds and grasses) now covers many of them and they have blended nicely into the river banks to become a long-term fixture. On some stretches, to improve marginal habitats, banks badly eroded ('poached') by cattle were fenced to allow riverside vegetation to re-grow.

The importance of monitoring outcomes

It may seem an obvious statement, but what is the point of doing extensive work on your fishery if you never know whether it has been successful or not? Small scale projects can be assessed by eye and from observations on the presence of fish or improved catches but bigger schemes need specialised monitoring to establish their outcomes. Positive results encourage further work whilst neutral or negative results are very valuable in telling us all what not to do in future - this is equally important. Nobody gets it all right all of the time - after all, the person who never made a mistake never made anything.

To assess the outcome of the Malmesbury Avon project the distribution and abundance of the various fish species was measured over each of the three study years (1996-1998) through electric-fishing surveys carried out by myself with the help of the Game Conservancy team. Also, I organised an annual catch record book scheme amongst keen Somerfords club members so that catches of all species could be related to weather, flows, stretches of river, etc. Both approaches delivered lots of valuable information. Electric-fishing is a lot of fun, you get to learn a great deal about exactly which habitats different fish species chose, how many fish live in given stretches and just how big they actually grow - really interesting. Of course, add to that the excitement of having done the experimental habitat improvements yourself, seeing whether it has worked, plus sharing the enthusiasm of club members watching to see whether fish numbers have increased and you have a really absorbing study. Remember that electric fishing needs EA approval in advance and must only be done by suitably qualified/experienced people.

Both improved stretches and adjacent controls (where no work had been done) were surveyed each year. Control sections should be essentially similar to experimental ones, save for the fact that nothing is done to them. Future monitoring then allows fair comparisons of results; if you have no controls you will never know whether raised fish numbers in experimental sections were due to your work or to other factors which have improved overall conditions in the river. You would be surprised how many projects are carried out with no controls and yet great claims are subsequently made for their success!

On average, over the three years, improved stretches supported: 3.8 times more barbel, 2.8 times more chub, 2.7 times more roach, 2.5 times more dace, 6 times more perch, and twice the number of gudgeon than the unimproved control stretches. Grayling numbers were 25 times higher in the improved stretches and wild brown trout also produced more parr - all in all, very encouraging results.

Clearly, for barbel, allied coarse species and for trout and grayling, the improved habitat stretches were consistently more attractive than the controls where no work had been done. The angling opportunities also increased through the provision of a series of new pools and these pools were fished actively, improving the recreational value of the river.

The yearly electric fishing surveys on the Malmesbury Avon also gave us useful fishery management information on habitat use by barbel and their growth and population structure.

Barbel population structure

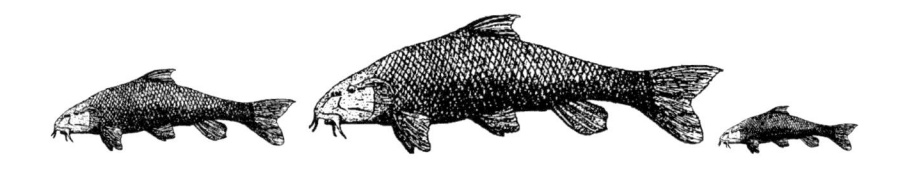

© Nick Giles

The barbel population contained an abundant sub-adult (10 to 25cm length) and adult (40-65cm length) population but a distinct lack of juveniles - fish of 0 to 2 years of age, less than 5cm long. In 1997 a single young-of-the-year barbel was caught and none in 1996 or 1998. This phenomenon of finding very few tiny barbel in UK fisheries surveys is common. The reasons may include:

1. That silt levels on gravel shallows are too high for successful egg incubation - silted eggs die from a lack of oxygen and are prone to fungal infections.
2. That river temperatures are generally too low for good barbel fry survival - chalk streams like the Hampshire Avon and limestone-fed rivers like the upper Bristol Avon may suffer particularly from this in high-flow summers when the cool aquifer water dominates temperature regimes. Barbel fry die at temperatures below 13 degrees C and prefer 15-18 degrees C.
3. That there is too little cover from the main current for young barbel fry during high flows, especially where livestock have poached banks, during floods or after bank-to-bank weed-cuts. This will be particularly true where flood defence dredging operations have previously ripped out most of the dead wood, tree roots, gravel bars, fringing vegetation, etc. Barbel up to 5cm prefer current speeds of around 5 body lengths per second and can just tolerate double this speed. Anything over 50cm per second will soon sweep fry away. Winter flows where shelter habitat is lacking may be particularly dangerous for young barbel and other coarse fish species.
4. That the nursery areas may often be relatively small and up side streams or on gravel shallows where the electric fishing surveys are not carried out.
5. That tiny barbel spread out along inner bank edges and are at a low density anyway, making them difficult to find. This is true, for instance, of young tench on still waters.
6. That, typically, most young-of-the-year barbel are eaten by bigger barbel and other predators. Open habitats may leave fry vulnerable to predation by chub and other species.
7. That the electric fishing gear is not adjusted to stun very small fish very efficiently and/or that they are often overlooked by the people with the collecting nets.

Clearly, much more research is needed before we know which, if any, of the above factors are the most important on given rivers. Given the value of barbel fisheries, such research work should be readily justifiable.

In UK rivers barbel grow relatively slowly but much more quickly in warmer, more southerly European rivers. Interestingly, in most fish, rapid growth tends to lead to a shorter life span and vice versa. The fishy equivalent of executive burn-out! Our laid-back British barbel prefer life in the slow lane - leading, potentially, to very long life spans. It isn't easy to find out just how long our barbel actually live - analyses of growth rings on the scales of specimen barbel produce large underestimates of true age. A scale which indicates an age of, say, 14 years could come from an ancient 34 year old which has been on 'tick-over' for twenty seasons, pushing all of its growth potential into annual egg production. Cane rod maestro Edward Barder often puts his bamboo creations through their paces on the Kennet which runs right past his Newbury workshop. In 2001 Edward caught a well known, easily-recognisable, crinkly-finned old barbel from the hole which it is known to have inhabited for many, many seasons. This low-double is reckoned to be pushing 40 years old and is still going strong! Should we be surprised at this when carp are known to live much longer? I think not. If global warming speeds up the growth rates of our barbel they will reach their maximum size earlier but, probably, die younger.

Habitat use

As expected from angling observations and radio-tracking of barbel elsewhere, the adult barbel of the Malmesbury Avon were usually recorded in deep glides and pools adjacent to some good cover structure (rock, tree roots, undercut banks or weed beds). The biggest fish tended to be seen and fished out of the deepest pools. Juvenile and maturing barbel were found thinly spread over shallower gravel-bedded sections. Our single barbel fry was found along a slack vegetated edge downstream of clean gravel spawning shallow, where the gravel had been scoured out by our upstream current deflectors and re-deposited (relatively silt-free) to form a fresh piece of spawning habitat.

These, then, are some of the key habitats which are critical to maintaining successful barbel fisheries. The good news is that, where natural river features have been destroyed, acceptable ones can be recreated at modest cost. It is crucial, however, to have a good overview of the river and to make new habitats where they are really needed and where no damage will be done to important existing habitats.

Higher up the Bristol Avon system, above the barbel zone, habitat restoration techniques which have worked well for me (and the wild trout and native crayfish) have included :

- Fencing out cattle which were breaking down banks and stripping vegetation bare.
- Building new gravel spawning shallows by tipping in and carefully profiling hundreds of tons of clean, suitably-sized gravel.
- Adding limestone boulder cover to shallows and glides.
- Planting new crowfoot beds.
- Coppicing alders, pollarding willows.
- Protecting banks with living willow and staked bundles of hazel twigs (faggots).

The success of this approach lies in recognising problems and applying cost-effective solutions in the right places on the river. Well-targeted habitat improvement is a potent way to improve both fishing performance and the sustainability of coarse and game fisheries.

Catch record books

A good way of gaining extra information on the success of the Malmesbury Avon project and of involving anglers directly in the work was issuing, collecting and analysing catch record books. Results showed how barbel catches varied from just above zero to nearly 3 per hour and that most fish were taken during fairly low summer flows. Barbel fishing was mostly done in pools like the Great Somerford weir pool (Duffer's hole') and in other artificial pools scoured by rock deflectors. Our new man-made pools provide both habitat for the adult barbel and productive places for anglers to fish.

The Yorkshire Swale

The upper reaches of Yorkshire's River Swale in the 1960s and early 1970s were famous for good mixed coarse fishing and particularly for barbel. In the 1970s a channelisation and flood management scheme robbed the river of many of its former fish-holding features, leaving long, relatively barren sections.

In recent years, however, hard work by the River Swale Preservation Society has improved the fishing markedly through the building of fish-holding features, planting willows and fencing out livestock which would otherwise strip the vegetation and trample the banks. The in-stream cover structures, built in the Pickhill, Holme and Ainderby areas, consisted of U-shaped stone-filled wire cages around two metres wide which deflect the current and provide shelter for fish hiding behind them. The key habitat feature created is, of course, shelter from the main force of the current, a critical factor in all river fisheries. Chub, in particular, love these shelters and good bags are regularly taken by legering next to these man-made 'feature pegs' which can produce forty pound hauls of prime chub.

This is a phenomenal improvement on a stretch where, two years before, matches were won with one or two chub and where there were many dry nets at the end of the afternoon. It would probably be possible to improve upon the materials used in this project - avoiding wire and using timber or natural rock structures and other natural materials. Most fisheries habitat improvement projects will be viewed more sympathetically by main-stream conservationists (including those in the Environment Agency who consent such works) if the materials used are natural and in keeping with the river stretch in question.

The River Perry

In 1978 Stephen Swales and Ken O'Hara decided to do some fish habitat improvement research on the River Perry, a tributary of the River Severn. The study stretch was gravel-bedded and around 8 metres wide. Previous land drainage works (deep-dredging) had removed most of the natural habitat features of shallow riffles, deeper pools and dead wood cover but weed growth was still abundant, giving the chub and dace plenty of cover in summer. In winter, however, when the weed died back and leaves fell from the trees, the fish were left vulnerable in a relatively bare open channel.

The 600 metre study section was split up into six equal stretches and combinations of low dams, current-deflectors and artificial cover structures were constructed along the middle four stretches whilst the upper-most and lower-most were left alone as 'controls'.

The key results of the River Perry study were :

The previously uniform, boring, dredged river channel was transformed into a better set of fish habitats with gravel shallows, deeper pools and with abundant shady cover. Overall, comparing fish densities in the year before the habitat improvements with the year after, dace numbers rose 75% (31% by weight) and chub increased 37% by number and 25% by weight. Had barbel been present, it is likely that they, too, would have responded positively.

Large concentrations of fish moved in right next to habitat structures - differing species found subtly different conditions which they preferred and took up residence accordingly. Physical cover structures were packed with fish; protection from potential predators is a key factor which fish need and which dredged rivers may totally lack. Just pinning a half log to the river bed with a gap underneath is often enough to attract fish. Before the habitat was improved the bigger chub on the Perry were effectively restricted to the few pools and areas of over-hanging vegetation missed by the dredging team. After the work was done, the chub and other species moved and spread out amongst the new wealth of varied habitats. What a lesson for fishery managers the world over!

Norfolk's River Wensum

The Norfolk Angler's Conservation Association (NACA) have a long and successful record of improving the Wensum. Long term damage had been caused by dredging - removing spawning shallows and other features and over-widening the channel. NACA took professional advice, got some plans drawn up, had them consented by the then NRA and got stuck in. New gravel shallows were built with suitable rock and gravel, trees were planted on eroding bends to reduce sediment inputs and create undercuts and a re-stocking programme used to kick-start the fishery. The restoration project has had its ups and downs - worries over flooding caused hiccups but these concerns were resolved. Relationships with the EA are good and collaborative work has been successful. An ever watchful eye needs keeping for pollution but roach fishing is on the up and fingers are crossed for specimen barbel fishing in seasons to come. Good for them, anglers improving the river for everyone's benefit. Locals have commented that the restored wavy channel with its shallows, pools and tree-lined undercuts looks 'just like it used to' - even better.

The point of citing these examples is to underline, for a range of species, the very positive results which can be achieved by well-targeted river habitat improvements on coarse (and game) fisheries. Clearly, this sort of work has enormous potential for improving the conservation value and angling quality on lowland coarse fisheries. An important point worth noting is that most studies of this type suffer from a lack of funding and are, necessarily, short-term. Given the economic importance of angling, this is dificult to understand. Research in the USA (where they have the vision to fund decent-sized fisheries research programmes) has shown that fish habitat improvements often have progressive long-term results - you can end up with a tremendous fishery if the habitat improvements are well-planned and implemented.

This sort of work need not be rocket science, often a simple fencing program can change a bare, over-wide, churned-up river section into a narrower, deeper weedy piece of prime fish habitat. A coil of wire, some staples, posts and elbow grease - not beyond the wit and resources of a typical fishing club winter working party. The work doesn't, however, stop there. If you don't manage the scrub and trees which soon grow, you can end up with a jungle. Continuous tweaking is the key - working a little and often to keep habitats in good shape, rather than letting things slide and then being faced with a huge amount of restoration work.

Of course, some areas of impenetrable jungle are good for fisheries....but not too much!

An important point to make is that you don't want to fence the whole of a stream. Some plant and invertebrate species need bare muddy areas to thrive and moderate grazing pressure often leads to high biodiversity - nice countryside to you and me. What is best for river and stream banks is variety - a mosaic of varied habitats harbouring as many species as possible.

It is important with habitat restoration to really raise the carrying capacity (number of fish which the stretch can support), rather than just moving around fish which you already have. The objective, then, is to develop high quality habitats for a wide range of aquatic wildlife, including self-sustaining fish stocks. Projects with the potential to improve habitats for rare species may attract funding from conservation agencies and other organisations and businesses wishing to generate positive public relations. Many barbel rivers are now designated as Sites of Special Scientific Interest (SSSIs) and a few as Special Areas of Conservation (SACs) - this recognition of their overall conservation value helps to generate funding for well-designed habitat improvement projects. All true anglers love to fish surrounded by dragonflies, mayflies, swallows, kingfishers, water voles, crayfish, water mint, crowfoot and willows. Mosquitoes are another thing altogether.

In summary - there is great scope for many more fisheries habitat improvement schemes on lowland rivers in the UK. It is important to take advice, designing works very carefully, to include habitat improvements for a range of aquatic wildlife, especially rare species (including fish) and to get Environment Agency consent before wading in!

Why not give it a try on your fishery; we have 25 years fisheries management experience and will be happy to discuss projects at no cost. Our contact details are inside the cover of this book.

Improving your barbel stretch

Given that you now know what barbel want in their habitat, you should be able to come up with some ideas for improving your fishery. Even small-scale initiatives can make a big difference. Remember to check with EA fishery staff whether formal consent is needed for your proposed works. Here are some simple and inexpensive ideas to get you started :

Idea 1 : Adding depth : dig some modest holes in the gravel bed in ideal spots for fishing and close by good beds of crowfoot, cabbages or bulrush. Once you have broken up the hard top layer, the gravel can be easily scooped downstream with a light weight shovel and raked to form a nice metre wide scoop, say 50cm deep and just a few metres long. Barbel tend to feed on the upstream slope of the scoop as this is where the current speed slows and food naturally collects. When properly sited in a brisk current these depressions will remain silt-free and can attract fish as soon as they are finished. One more barbel swim on your fishery.

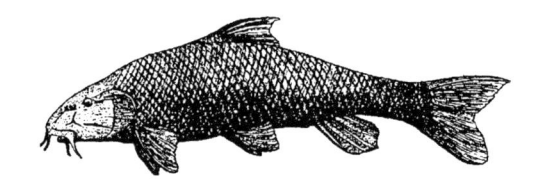

Idea 2 : Adding cover : carefully site some large boulders in a deep run which is otherwise devoid of cover. Boulders form a slack water area at their downstream edge, perfect for fish to hide behind and with the added advantage that food drifting in the current (hemp, worms, maggots, shrimps, nymphs, etc) is 'sucked in' to form a natural larder for the fish which is snug in its hidey hole. A half log pinned close above the bed will soon attract fish, especially if it is securely staked along the edge and close to a pool and gravel shallows.

Winter-planted willow shoots positioned over deep glides and on the eroding side of bends should root at or around the waterline, developing excellent swims with cover above and the potential for the formation of an undercut bank below. Alder and willow root masses in clay banks on the outside of bends often promote the formation of deep undercuts which are much-used by barbel, chub and trout for daytime cover. Keep bankside trees and shrubs pollarded or coppiced on a 5 year cycle so as to avoid over-shading and rotting. Retain bank protection and fish cover with the root masses. Fish shelters can also be made by tethering floating branches to the bank over deep fast runs which lack cover. These soon build up floating scum and debris to form excellent chub and barbel haunts.

Logs and root wads can be securely pinned to the river bed. It is amazing how quickly fish take advantage of any new physical cover provided for them. It is a sad fact that, on today's over-managed river banks, there tends to be a dearth of natural deadwood cover which is so necessary for wary fish to feel safe and take up residence. A fishery with abundant good cover will attract and hold wandering fish looking for the best available habitat, the fishing will improve accordingly. Also, by siting your cover structures cleverly, you can attract fish to live throughout the fishery, making the maximum use of the available water and reducing pressure on a small number of existing 'hot spot' swims.

Make certain that your in-stream structures can't float away and block bridges or sluices - this can cause damage to structures and increase flood risk. Take expert advice on your overall plan and make sure all necessary consents are in hand before you start work.

Idea 3 : Adding comfort : the equivalent to a comfy armchair for a fish is shelter from strong currents. Water is viscous, it drags on the body of a fish, pulling it along with the current and making a fish work to maintain its station. For instance, water at 7 degrees C is twice as viscous as at 20 Degrees C and so the effort of swimming against a current is much greater in winter than in summer. Winter also, of course, tends to bring strong flows and high water conditions, further adding to the barbel's problems.

Shelter can be provided by a rock, tree-trunk or carefully sited current deflector. These can be made from hazel or willow hurdles, bundles of twigs (faggots) or similar materials, supported on wooden posts driven well into the bed so as to push the current out from the bank. I recommend simple temporary structures using natural materials which are easy and cheap both to make and move, should their siting prove to be wrong.

Habitat in-crease

When you get a current-deflector right, you will form that zone of differing current speeds so beloved of barbel, chub, roach, trout and many other species : the crease. A crease is a visible surface ripple with faster water on the mid-stream side and a slower current towards the bank. The zone of differing current speeds can go right down to the river bed in many instances. Fish sit on the edge of the crease in the more comfortable slacker current, moving out into the faster current to intercept passing food items. Creases are especially attractive if they incorporate the right depth, current diversion and overhead cover for the species which you are trying to encourage. You can make creases just like the ones which naturally form where side streams flow in, where scour holes form eddies or where a fallen tree trunk lies out from the bank at an angle to the current. Barbel soon find these little areas of better habitat and take up residence. More good swims on your fishery.

Idea 4 - Better spawning and nursery habitat

Trout and salmon stocks have been increased through improved recruitment by de-silting spawning gravels - this can be done by forking over gravel in small streams or by high pressure water-jetting over larger areas. Take care not to cloud the waters for downstream neighbours who may not appreciate it; work together to clean up riffles over a considerable length of water, starting at the upstream end and working down. This could help barbel in silty rivers if done during (say) April, just before the normal spawning period. But, be careful - check with your local Environment Agency fisheries officer to make sure that no harm will be done to other species living on the gravel shallows or to water quality. For instance, there may be salmon or trout fry or lamprey or bullhead eggs incubating in gravels on some rivers where you are trying to improve conditions for barbel. Lampreys, in particular, are now of considerable conservation interest across Europe and salmon are getting pretty scarce in many catchments. Don't forget that gravel cleaning is really a 'sticking plaster' solution to high levels of siltation. What is actually needed is better land use practice along river catchments, eg buffer-zoning and stock fencing, to stop the silt getting in there in the first place.

A more ambitious project to improve spawning habitats is to build some new gravel bars on the bed of the river. These must be made the right shape and placed correctly so that they work properly and do not divert flows in the wrong way - perhaps scouring banks, creating too much erosion or increased flood risk. Gravel of the wrong size in the wrong place can also be swept away by winter floods. Take advice, if you need it, the costs should be recouped over the years with a more self-sustaining fishery attracting better incomes and needing less stocking.

When seeking advice, beware of the instant expert - an 'ex' is a has-been and a spurt is a drip under pressure!

Stocking

Many barbel fisheries have been established by initial stocking and some need successive batches of fish to maintain catches. Whilst it is usually best to improve fisheries via creating better quality habitats - self-sustaining fisheries, sometimes stocking with young barbel can make a big and cost-effective difference to angling performance. The EA have recently stocked 4,500 young barbel into the Thames between Marlow and Kingston - this in response to anglers' wishes to catch more barbel. Good for the EA. A similar scheme on the Medway in Kent has proved similarly popular with the locals. Many Wensum specimens were originally stocked as youngsters by the Norfolk Anglers Conservation Association. Yorkshire's River Don around Doncaster received 6000 young barbel five or six years ago. Even as famous a barbel river as the middle and lower Hampshire Avon has recently been stocked with hundreds of 20cm plus barbel, they should survive well but will they breed successfully?

Talking this over a while ago with Pete Reading (renowned barbel angler and Chairman of Christchurch Angling Club), we concluded that, maybe, a cool fast river like the Avon is, in most years, just too cold and inhospitable for young barbel to thrive in. Perhaps the Avon barbel stocks that we do have, including good numbers of large fish, were produced mostly in warm low-flow years when higher than usual river temperatures and low current speeds boosted fry survival. At Somerley small stream (carrier) systems off the main river have, over recent seasons, been given some good management treatment and the fishery now benefits from large shoals of young cyprinid fish. Whether barbel have used these areas to the same extent as roach, chub and dace I don't know but the habitat is there for them to find. This sort of side stream improvement has a valuable role to play on many rivers.

If barbel behave like chub and dace, runs of wet cold years will have long-term negative impacts on fisheries whilst runs of drier, warmer summers will boost stocks. Stocking could, in the right circumstances, make all the difference to the future prospects and performance of the fishery if we have long runs of cool summers. Also, where large numbers of spawning shallows have been removed or major weirs block migration routes, stocking may be the most cost-effective or even the only way of boosting fishery performance on stretches isolated from good habitat. Sometimes stocking can be combined with habitat improvements whilst, at other sites, habitat improvements alone can produce self-sustaining coarse fish stocks. Each fishery needs individual consideration.

Fishery improvement plans

Let's have a brief recap. Electric-fishing surveys or catch records tend to show up rivers with poor barbel recruitment and these may be the best waters to consider for habitat improvement or judicious stocking programmes. Fish stocked into rivers need prior Environment Agency 'Section 30' consents and habitat improvements may need EA 'Flood Defence' consents. Introductions of modest numbers of health-certified young barbel can even-out natural year class fluctuations and provide fisheries with a good range of barbel sizes. Habitat improvement can also help, for instance, building new gravel spawning shallows or cleaning up existing ones at the right time of year. Improving deep water lies and physical cover provide further opportunities for fisheries improvement producing better angling opportunities and barbel growth and survival.

The best starting point for planning fishery improvements is to carefully draw a fishery map, noting existing features and sketching in proposed new ones. Try to visualise what is missing, as well as what is actually there. There is tremendous scope for the planting of bank side shrubs, fencing out livestock where necessary, construction of new cover, river-bed scoops, current-deflectors and all sorts of other ideas. It is quite beyond me why more clubs / fishery owners don't take a fresh look at what they are offering both the anglers and their fish by way of attracting them to their waters. The results can be startlingly good and the work need not be expensive to carry out. Expert advice helps enormously and saves time and wasted expense in the long-run.

In this chapter we have seen how coarse fisheries respond to better habitats - they improve; under optimal conditions, they thrive. We have also seen that virtually all fisheries have scope for habitat improvement and that this is often quite straightforward. Careful habitat improvement can create better fish stocks and better opportunities for high quality angling experiences. This experience isn't necessarily a bigger personal best fish but, simply, greater enjoyment of a pleasant, diverse, natural place to cast your bait and sit back in quiet contemplation.

The next chapter takes what we have learned about barbel biology, habitats and fisheries and describes successful approaches to fishing for barbel using techniques both old and new.

© Clare Yates

CHAPTER

5

Ecological coarse fishing

MGN Ltd

'Fishing is different from all other things. It is concerned with so much more than just physical facts; the centre of it is really a state of mind'.

Bernard Venables : Freshwater Fishing.

Ecological coarse fishing - is an approach to angling which involves an understanding of river ecology - reading the water and fish behaviour, choosing the right swim in the right weather conditions at the right time of day, using the right bait on the right tackle to catch fish which you haven't already scared. And then returning them, undamaged.

The geographical range of barbel fishing in the UK has increased in recent decades, with more river fisheries available to large numbers of anglers at modest prices. Some sections of the Bristol Avon, Dorset

Stour, Trent, Thames and Kennet, for instance, offer free urban fishing - all you need is a rod licence. Club membership brings excellent, affordable barbel fishing within the reach of most anglers. Birmingham Anglers Association with good stretches of the Severn and Teme is a good example of a low-cost set-up offering excellent fishing quite close to major cities. You don't need posh tackle to catch barbel and bait can be collected for free with a little effort. The more you put into your fishing, the more you should get back out. Whilst always being fairly popular with 'father & son' anglers, barbel fishing has, in the last ten to fifteen years, become in-vogue with specialist anglers who really value the subtleties and challenges of the sport. At this end of the financial spectrum, for those with ready access to top-of-the-range tackle, personal transport and able to afford syndicate membership fees, there are many relatively exclusive barbel stretches. Rivers such as the Hampshire Avon, Dorset Stour, Great Ouse, Wye, Kennet and Severn offer stretches with big fish, relative solitude, peace and tranquillity. It's a great way to forget the pressures of work, mortgages, keeping the kids on the straight and narrow, mowing the lawn, decorating and servicing the car. Exclusive fishing is fine but I hope that not too many stretches go that way - coarse fishing should be available to all at modest cost.

The Barbel Society

Recent growth of the Barbel Society reflects the popularity of the species, especially amongst specimen hunters and specialist anglers. The Society was formed at a meeting of 32 keen barbellers held at Upton upon Severn in April 1995, they elected Peter Stone as the first President. A fine choice. After only two years membership topped a thousand and waters on the Severn and Teme had been leased for members, a stretch of the Bristol Avon at Chippenham has recently been added. The current President is Fred Crouch and the enthusiastic and hard-working Steve Pope chairs the committee. If you are interested in joining, membership details are available from : John Found,158 Douglas Road, Tolworth, Surbiton, Surrey, KT6 7SE, Tel 0181 399 4543. If you are a web surfer, have a look at www.thebarbelsociety.com.

Dave Burr, editor of the Barbel Soc. magazine, kindly penned the following for me:

Why Barbel?

What is it about this particular species of fish that so captivates me? I have been, if not obsessed, pretty well focused on other fish at different times. I've chased carp, pike, roach, tench and even bream with unhealthy vigour, so why am I now a confirmed barbel nut?

Could it be that barbel frequent our most beautiful rivers? For many years I have made do with sitting on the banks of lakes, slow-moving rivers and dour drains, each with its own beauty. But now I come alive when I am next to or stood in a swift flowing, clear river where the air is filled with the music of it's movement, accompanied by the sounds of nature.

Maybe it's the 'hunter gatherer' in me. I have a deep-seated need to hunt. I cannot explain it but I think that all specialist anglers will understand. Barbel fishing enables me to apply my hunting skills to the full whether it is through stalking or by laying an ambush.

Is it the bite? That electrifying moment, when after a few knocks and tremors, the rod is wrenched around by that unseen force. No other British fish can come close to providing that thrill; it is as addictive as any drug.

Or the fight? The powerful runs, the dogged determination of a fish reluctant to leave the sanctuary of the riverbed. Then, just when you think it's all over and you bring an apparently beaten barbel to the net, they always have the energy for one, two or even three desperate lunges for freedom.

It could be that moment when you lay your fish on the unhooking mat, unfold the mesh of your landing net and gaze upon the most splendid of creatures. The bullish profile, the magnificent fins tinged in coral pink. The neat scale pattern. The green and gold. How rare to find deformities, each fish 'fresh from the packet'.

To quote Trefor West, *'Every one is a prize'*.

Thanks Dave.

Barbel fishing

THE BARBEL GOES OFF WITH A HEAVY RUSH, BORING DEEP

© MGN Ltd

The specialist approach to barbel fishing essentially involves joining a society, syndicate or good club, learning the location of productive swims, baiting them up with a bait which the barbel haven't learned to avoid and using rigs and approaches which maximise your chances of success. Barbel aren't too smart at recognising novel foods and, where angling pressure is low and little bait goes in, barbel may often be difficult to tempt immediately with off-the-shelf pellets, boilies and exotic pastes. Educated barbel are, however, a completely different story - these fish will learn to accept some weird baits but can be really difficult to catch unless you stay one step ahead of them in the tactics race. This is especially the case where food competition is low and fish can afford to be choosy. Certain old favourites such as hemp, casters, maggots and luncheon meat, however, may carry on being successful over long periods. Maybe many barbel just can't resist them; particles like hemp, in particular, being capable of tempting these fish to feed with confidence even where angling pressure is high.

Trefor West and Tony Miles (Quest for Barbel, Crowood) believe that confident barbel will feed on most baits and that making sure that you haven't scared the fish is the key factor for success- who am I to argue with these guys? I suspect that much depends upon local circumstances and on an intimate knowledge of the fishery. Like carp, many barbel probably don't need to be caught very often on a given bait before they learn to treat it with suspicion. There will always be exceptions, of course, and, on 'hungry' rivers where food competition is high, barbel may have to take more risks to get enough to eat.

Archie Braddock was the pioneer of flavoured baits on rivers, trying loads of novel combinations on his beloved Trent before developing consistently successful blends. Many have followed in his footsteps, for instance, John Baker products are very popular with carp and barbel anglers alike. A good feature of bait development and the wide taste-range of barbel is that, rather than paying high prices for specialist base mixes and additives, you can, if you have time, mix up your own from cheap, readily available products. Trial and error with various mixes will gradually teach you what works, where and when. Pet shops, corner stores, supermarkets - all have shelves full of prospective barbel baits. Whether these are as good as the specialist products seems to be a matter of widely differing opinions, I leave it up to you to 'pay yer money and take yer choice'.

With a wealth of natural food plus a cornucopia of angler's baits and warmer summers in prospect, specimen barbel are now turning up in a wide range of rivers. All you need to catch them is water craft plus the right tackle, bait and approach - read on.

Baits

To say that barbel have catholic tastes in food is an understatement. Key baits and ground baits include : hemp, maize, wheat, maple peas, tiger nuts, peanuts, trout pellets, carp pellets, halibut pellets, bread crumb, bread flake, crust, 'luncheon' meats, Bacon Grill, garlic sausage, sausage meat, prawns, shrimps, cockles, mussels, lob worm (and other worms), cheese paste, maggots / casters, commercially mixed special pastes/boilies, Campbell's meat balls in various flavours, …..there's no shortage of offerings to experiment with. Much depends on how keen you are, how much money you are willing to spend on bait and whether you have the time and resources to pre-bait swims regularly.

I don't propose to talk too much about specialist baits as they are pretty well-known anyway and other books (eg by John Baker, Andy Orme, Roger Miller and John Wilson) already do a better job than I can on the subject. High-tech baits may give you the edge where barbel are canny and under pressure, currently a small boilie with paste moulded around it, fished on a hair rig is the state of the art. This approach has sorted out the recent record fish - the paste dissolves slowly leaving a taste trail for barbel to home in on. Even when the paste has all gone, the boilie is still sitting there - very neat and effective. These intensively tested baits and associated flavourings certainly work, but, they aren't cheap - especially if you go in for mega-pre-baiting programs. Fear not - you can be a successful barbel fisher without taking out a second mortgage to buy bait.

A common feature of angler behaviour is trying to copy the success of others, rather than thinking for yourself. This is fine if that's what you want to do - I'm not knocking it. Many anglers don't have the time or inclination to experiment with various baits. There is, however, another road to success. Develop your own ideas - use affordable ingredients and try them now and again as change baits so that you don't get fed-up with too many blank sessions. Try using two rods with differing baits when things are slow. You may just hit on a really good new bait which, if you keep it under your hat (not literally), will serve you well in the long term. The first guy to try a few grains of sweet corn or a chunk of Bacon Grill must have been pleased with the results! Alternatively, rather than concocting the latest flavoured boilie or paste or raiding Tescos for every can in sight, you may like to try a natural bait. They are free and fun to collect.

Natural baits

The thought of using natural baits for barbel isn't a recent one :

'Obviously we ought to fish for barbel with the things that they eat normally..........If I had a private barbel swim I'd make all sorts of experiments..........

I believe that water-snails and fresh-water shrimps, and things like that, are the barbel's natural food. The trouble is putting them on the hook. Shrimps are tiny little things, and barbel hooks have to be pretty stout in the wire. Perhaps you could use some sticky stuff like seccotine and simply stick four or five shrimps to the hook. Snails might be tied on with fine thread. Frenchmen use aniseed cake for many kinds of fish, and they tie it to their hooks with thread. They call it 'la noquette'. We don't know everything about fishing in England, though we think we do'

                H.T.Sherringham, Coarse Fishing (1912).

Good old Sherringham, demonstrating to us that hair rigs and bait glues have been around for longer than we might have thought.

All barbel start off on natural foods although, on heavily-fished rivers, they are probably weaned onto maggots, hemp, meat and corn at an early age. Even these fish, however, won't stop eating natural foods. Normally, we ground bait to educate barbel into eating something which they haven't been caught on much before or which they know about but need some free offerings to get them feeding confidently. Added attractions for most anglers are that the bait is reasonably cheap, easy to buy and use. Pre-baiting takes time, effort & further money but can make a big difference to catches.

Hang on a minute though, why not use the river as your natural ground-baiter - it's full of invertebrates which the fish are used to eating with no worries about being caught. Why not wade around a bit in some safe shallow areas with a firm bed, shuffling your feet to send a stream of natural food downstream towards your barbel swim. Follow that up by using some of the bigger, juicier invertebrates for bait, either under a float or lightly legered. Obviously, we don't want to switch barbel off their natural food by having them associate invertebrates with danger. But, by using a restricted range of the bigger species, there are still dozens of smaller ones which barbel can eat and which will never be useful for bait - barbel will never starve. Also, the ways in which we anglers present invertebrates as bait (in open water) are very different from the places barbel usually expect to find these foods under natural conditions (largely buried between and under the gravel). So the fish may not learn to avoid them when feeding naturally anyway. Natural baits should often succeed with little or no pre-baiting and with barbel from both heavily- and lightly-fished waters.

Which invertebrates can you readily collect that will be good for bait, I hear you ask? Here are some suggestions - there is great scope for experimentation.

Firstly, there are natural baits which you can collect in the garden or buy quite cheaply at the local tackle shop or fishmongers - worms, slugs, leatherjackets (crane fly larvae), maggots and casters, shrimps, prawns, cockles, etc. Maggots do, of course, occur naturally and fish may well come across them if, for instance, a fly-blown dead sheep is lying in the shallows. Much to my amusement an angling chum wandered into a ripe one of these hanging on a tree on the banks of the Wye; he was trying to keep his feet on a slippery clay bank after floods and blundered straight into it - little sympathy was shown for his plight!

Less you forget - you can go worm-chasing on village greens, sports fields and lawns after dusk on warm wet evenings with a dull torch and a strong back. Be prepared to explain this behaviour to the local constable. Or, you could pretend to get interested in gardening and dig over the garden. Wormeries are well worth cultivating under the disguise of 'a useful compost heap'. For you Rambos out there, dig up some wasp nests and grab the cakes full of grubs - good luck! Before maggots were so readily available, wasp grubs were a regular bait when trotting for chub. Slugs are easier to collect and they don't sting. Or, you could stroll down to the fishmonger and get hold of some freshly cooked cockles - well worth a go. Cockles, by the way, are ace baits for both tench and carp.

Or, there are natural baits which can easily be collected from the water side. These include caddis larvae, alder fly (*Sialis*) larvae, large (*Ephemera*) mayfly nymphs, stone fly nymphs, snails, mussels, and others. A few words about some of the key possibilities are appropriate here:

Caddis grubs

Caddis grubs (larvae) are a traditional but now little-used natural bait. Many early authors recommend 'cad' bait, some rating it the best of offerings for barbel. They can be collected either from the bottoms of stones in the shallows or with a pond net from gravelly shallows and silty/weedy river margins. Both cased and uncased species make good baits and are a mainstream part of the natural diet of barbel. To obtain some naturals, try wading on a gravel shallow, pushing a net vertically down onto the bed just downstream of you and then shuffling your boots for a minute or two. In your net - you will be amazed at the numbers of shrimps, caddis larvae, small mussels and nymphs which you have dislodged. These are the beasts that barbel go foraging for at dawn and dusk when they head off to the shallows on their regular feeding sprees. What better baits could you ask for? Pop them in a bucket of cool water and off you go. Only keep what you need and release the rest. Return immediately any native crayfish or lamprey larvae. Try deep-trotting, light legering or trundling the commoner large invertebrates for barbel, chub, specimen roach and other species. If wading in rivers isn't your idea of fun, mealworms, available from some pet shops are a caddis alternative recommended by Steve Stayner.

Shrimps

On clean chalk streams and limestone-based rivers shrimps can be large and very abundant, especially in areas where rotting twigs and leaves accumulate. On the Hampshire Avon, where I do most of my fishing, shrimps are everywhere and must be an important food source for barbel. Large shrimps are easy to catch and make good baits for virtually all fish species. Give them a try, they are around on many rivers in enough numbers to make this a reasonable option.

Pea mussels

Swan mussels are a traditional carp and tench bait - they also catch barbel. Pea mussels are much smaller (finger nail sized) and can occur in silty margins and over more gravelly areas. These molluscs are readily taken by many bottom-feeding fish. On stillwaters they are a particular favourite food of tench and carp. I'm sure barbel would happily mop them up given the chance - certainly, they will not associate them with the danger of being caught. Cooked cockles look just like the insides of pea mussels - maybe this is why they are so attractive to tench, in particular.

Alder fly larvae

Alder flies (*Sialis*) have big meaty predatory larvae which live amongst silty leaf litter, hunting smaller invertebrates, catching them in their pincer-like jaws and swallowing them whole. As revealed by the stomach contents of Mr Cassey's 16lb Hampshire Avon barbel - they are on the menu of very big fish indeed. Once you have learned to catch them in a pond net (or fine-meshed landing net) swished through the surface silt layer along river margins, off you go. Try two or three bunched on a size 10 - they are a very attractive bait. Around Easter time you may notice adult alder flies on the wing, they are almost black, 2-3cm long with long antennae and shiny wings folded down the back like the apex of a roof. Adult alders are taken by trout, and probably by chub too.

Mayfly nymphs

The 'angler's mayfly', *Ephemera danica* and similar species have large pale yellow nymphs which burrow into the silt around the base of water crowfoot beds and in gravelly shallows. These insect larvae usually live underwater for two years before emerging as adult flies. Shuffling your boots around the base of weed beds with a fine-meshed net held just downstream is a good way to catch them - they occur on most barbel rivers. These things are wizard baits for a great range of fish, being large, juicy and conspicuous. I have caught some cracking roach whilst trotting them on fine tackle. As mentioned above, not many anglers will have gone to the trouble that you have to collect them for bait so you have a head start over the guys who are still peddling sweet corn and pork luncheon meat cubes.

Stonefly nymphs

Most stonefly species are found in more upland and spatier rivers than *Ephemera* mayflies. The big dark nymphs are called 'creepers' and are traditionally used on fly tackle, fished downstream for canny wild brown trout. Barbel will wolf them down too, especially if presented on fine float gear.

Crayfish

Traditionally, our native white-clawed crayfish was used extensively as a chub and barbel bait. Now this species is rare and protected by law - don't even think about using them, they are too precious for that. The introduced larger, red-clawed, North American Signal crayfish is also now on the prowl in many of our waters. These mini-lobsters are taking over river catchments in a big way, the Bristol Avon, Kennet and Great Ouse, for instance. They can transmit a deadly crayfish plague to our native crays, causing widespread wipe-outs of stocks (this has happened on both the Hampshire Avon and the Dorset Stour) and they probably also out-compete native crays for food and space, even when no fungal plague spores are present. For this reason their use as bait is banned by byelaw in England and Wales - in fact, as far as I know, no crayfish species can now be used legally for bait.

Signal crays burrow deeply into banks, causing erosion and leaks, they eat vast numbers of snails, other invertebrates, fish spawn and small fish and they pinch our baits. The swines can even mimic barbel bites - clearly, this is war! Signal crays probably represent a big new food resource for many freshwater fish and may be partly responsible for the fast growth of specimen chub and barbel on some rivers. Whatever you do, however, don't be tempted to move Signals or any other crayfish around from river to river or between lakes as you may introduce crayfish plague to new locations with disastrous results for any resident native crayfish populations and for the fishery in general.

Fish

Minnows

© Clare Yates

Minnows are a noted early season barbel bait. These days, live-baiting is regarded by many as an unacceptable angling practice - a very valid point of view. In the light of this, if you want to use fish for bait at all, it is well worth considering the use of small dead baits for barbel. These should be caught and used on the same fishery, not transferred between rivers. Minnows, freshly and humanely killed, can make an excellent barbel bait and are well worth a try through the early summer. Consider this quote from Patrick Chalmers writing in the 1930s :

> 'But the minnows, to see him, crowd all against the sheathing in a cloud. And the barbel, coming close, opens his mouth and seems to suck into it a tithe of the school. He seems to inhale minnows, rather than catch them. And then he lounges on his way. '

Lampreys

Whilst, because of their conservation status, we should not use lamprey larvae (ammocoetes) for bait, it is perfectly alright to use sections of dead sea/river lamprey sold frozen for pike fishing. Lamprey flesh has a smell and texture which is very attractive to many predatory fish - it was a noted barbel bait, for instance, a hundred years ago on the Trent when fish up to 16 pounds 10 ounces are recorded as being caught on lamprey-baited night lines. Clearly, the days of night-lining for barbel for the pot are gone but the use of lampreys which have been collected dead and dying after spawning poses no threat to the species and provides some good bait. Catching pre-spawning lampreys on their way upstream is another matter, however, and it may be worth bait companies checking their sources. No true angler wants to threaten the survival of any species through his or her activities. I've seen stag beetle larvae recommended as angling baits - these, too, are rare and best left alone. Fishing doesn't need to make problems for itself by provoking criticism from main stream conservationists. Not when there are so many harmless barbel baits freely available.

Peter Wheat (in The Fighting Barbel) mused that, because spawning lampreys become attached to each other by their toothy suckers and covered in cuts, they may well attract barbel by the smell of their blood in the water. Peter may well be right here - barbel will certainly investigate a free meal of meaty lamprey on the gravel shallows. After all, lampreys spawn and then die in just the areas that barbel patrol for food every night. What could be more natural than barbel scavenging on their corpses?

Too busy?

If the time and trouble of collecting natural baits seems just too great, worry not. Most barbel currently get caught on a short-list of tried and tested offerings - this is even true of the biggest ones on the hardest-pressed waters.

What baits catch double figure barbel?

Andy Orme (Barbel Mania) reviewed big barbel catches reported to Angler's Mail in 1987-89, noting the most popular baits which they were caught on. Most of these double figure fish were taken on luncheon meat (36%), maggots/casters (32%) and sweetcorn (9%). A chum of mine (Nick Bubb) recently gave me a 5-year run of Angler's Mails which he had squirrelled away in the corner of his bedroom (his poor wife). This gave me the opportunity to scan through them to see whether big barbel are now coming out on different baits to those in vogue around 15 years ago. I looked at the years 1997 and 2000, picking out around a hundred double figure fish at random in each year and noting the baits they were caught on.

In 1997 luncheon meat scored 35%, maggots/casters 39%, corn 14%, pastes/boilies 8%, plus a few barbel on worm, meatball, swan mussel, and cheese.

In 2000 Luncheon meat scored 41%, pastes/boilies 32%, maggots/casters 10%, corn 9%, plus a few on trout pellets, meatballs, worm and cheese.

The rivers which produced these fish were the Great Ouse 18%, Kennet 15%, Hampshire Avon 13%, Bristol Avon 7%, Trent 7%, Severn, Wye, Dorset Stour and Warwick Avon all on 5% with a few from the Ribble, Wharfe, Lee, Loddon, Colne, Thames, Wey, Teme, Dove and Swale. A good broad range of rivers.

What can we conclude from a brief survey like this? Probably not too much but it is interesting to note that :

- Specialist pastes and boilies have now moved from the carp scene into the barbel swim - the many years of development of carp baits can now be applied successfully to barbel fishing.

- Luncheon meat and corn still account for around the same

percentage of big barbel as they did 15 years ago but now they are often flavoured and/or coloured. Maggots / casters seem to have dropped off in popularity, despite their ready availability. This may well be down to cost - they aren't exactly cheap.

- Trout pellets and meat balls are catching a few good quality barbel, but the traditional cheese paste, bread flake and worm have sunk in popularity, more or less, without trace!

Of course, very many big barbel are never reported to the angling press and some anglers keep baits pretty much a secret or even give false leads on successful ones (devious devils). Make of it what you will but bear in mind that pastes and boilies are probably here to stay on many of our barbel rivers. Maybe it's ground-baiting with these highly nutritious foods which has helped some barbel on heavily fished stretches grow so big in recent years. 'The Pope' - the record barbel during summer 2001 weighed 19lb but was caught two years before (at the same time of year) at 16lb 13oz. Steve Pope (Barbel Society Chairman), after whom, apparently, the fish was cheekily named, reckons that this sort of weight gain is principally down to the large quantities of boilies going into the Great Ouse each season - he may well be right. It's an interesting thought of Fred Crouch's that barbel actually seem to do best where they are fished for - after all, they get hand-fed there. So much for the 'antis'.

Once you have decided on your favoured bait, you may need some help with fishing methods. The next section summarises some productive approaches to barbel angling.

Fishing methods for barbel

© MGN Ltd

'I would never fish if I thought that I could not return what I catch, unharmed, to the river'

Andy Orme, Barbel Mania.

Well said Andy; here are a few successful approaches developed by experienced barbel fishers. Don't be afraid to try new methods of your own - you may surprised how well you do. One thing's for sure, if you just copy everyone else on your fishery, you are unlikely to out-wit even your average barbel much of the time. Big ones are less likely again to be fooled. It's worth re-capping on some fundamental tips at this stage:

Take a stealthy wander before choosing your swim, you may see a shoal of barbel and so greatly increase your chances of success.

Keep quiet and keep out of sight when approaching your swim. Don't scare your fish.

Study the fish-holding features in your chosen stretch. Barbel often pack into small areas such as scoops in the river bed or under logs, undercuts, rock gulleys, etc and taking zones can often be very small.

Barbel often use traditional routes to travel from safe cover to feeding areas, these often follow the deepest available water or run close to sheltering weeds, undercuts, etc. Cast into the hot spot and get a bite, miss the key area and you may as well cast your bait into the field behind you, accurate location can make that much difference, especially with big fish.

Serial swim-hopping/Roving

Winter

This approach, used very successfully by Tony Miles and Trefor West, involves walking a stretch slowly and carefully, reading the water and noting likely swims. Each swim is then baited up with hemp and allowed to settle down. This phase is vital as fishing a swim too soon can easily spook wary fish. By giving the barbel plenty of time to settle on the hemp and free offerings, you can steal up quietly on a swim with confidently feeding fish. As big barbel take the longest time to settle but then muscle out smaller ones, this is a good way of contacting specimen fish. Leave the swims too long, however, and the bulk of the feed will be eaten and the fish will have moved on. Or, someone else will have hopped in to take advantage of your hard work. Experience helps get the timing right.

The baited swims are usually fished by downstream legering, until either a fish or two is caught or nothing happens for quite a while, at which point a move is made to the next pre-baited spot. This approach is very good for locating fish in swollen, turbid, warm winter spates when barbel often feed like mad but can be difficult to find. In winter, on most barbel rivers, there are far fewer anglers than in the summer and there are usually plenty of swims available to bait up without fear of them being 'poached'. Baits can vary from a couple of grains of corn or hookful of maggots to a cube of Bacon Grill or a whopping two or three Campbell's Meat Balls which can be dynamite in the right circumstances. On harder fished waters the specialist paste/boilie combination is an alternative approach.

A useful tip when downstream touch-legering is to hold a slack loop of line in your fingers and to let it go when you feel a stealthy draw from a barbel, this can allay the fish's fears by stopping it feeling any resistance. It's a bit similar to the loop of line which the salmon fly fisherman gives a fish, rather than striking too soon at the sight or feel of a take.

By fishing swims in rotation a considerable bag of good fish can be amassed, no single swim is 'hammered', interest is maintained by fishing a variety of swims and the chances of finding a group of feeding barbel is greatly increased. The alternative of choosing a good looking spot and sitting it out resolutely for hours overlooks the key point that, despite appearances, there may not be any feeding fish in residence! This happens all too often. How many times have I done this myself?

Summer/autumn roving

The summer/autumn equivalent of this approach has been well documented by Andy Orme, Roger Miller and John Bailey (see reading list). The roving approach is still central but, rather than baiting up a series of swims, the anglers goes 'walk-about', fish-spotting with a minimum of tackle and fishing for spotted specimens. Long experience, for instance, on the River Wye has taught these very successful anglers that many good looking 'barbel swims' actually fail to hold fish with any consistency. Also, some swims which do hold barbel hardly ever yield them to the angler. Tim Pryke was recently fishing the Wye during the tail-end of the Foot and Mouth disease outbreak when access to the river was severely restricted owing to the beef cattle production regime on local farms. Tim was, therefore, forced to fish several swims which he (or anyone else) had ignored in the past as they looked pretty hopeless. The result was 47 barbel in ten days, many of these fish were sheltering under near-bank vegetation (Himalayan balsam) which had grown up owing to a lack of fishing pressure. Tim reckons that we need to re-assess what barbel really are looking for in a swim - maybe these fish use much greater areas of the river than we realise. If we all keep on fishing the well known and obvious holding spots, we won't learn much that's new will we? As usual, Tim has a good point.

By forsaking some mid-day fishing (while the sun is high in the sky) it is possible to get a good idea of barbel distribution by very careful fish-watching. Some tree climbing or crawling through nettles/

cow pats will be required; no gain without pain! The observations are then coupled with early morning or dusk sessions, sometimes with natural baits and fishing from unusual pitches (eg in chest-waders from big boulders, rock ledges, etc) where stealthy specimens can be taken unawares. Barbel feed confidently where they are not used to being caught and on food items which they do not associate with danger. Use of caddis larvae, lob worms, dead minnows, etc for bait and presenting that bait in a lie not readily accessible to the usual bank anglers can lead to instant success and a lot of satisfaction. Implicit in this approach is the spreading out of angling pressure and the maintenance of a well conditioned and not overly-stressed barbel stock. Field craft, reading the river and stealth are all central to success.

Tony Miles has developed a method where he uses low-concentration flavoured boilies for pre-baiting to get barbel used to a particular taste. This is followed up with an angling session with more strongly flavoured bait and no free offerings - the static small boilie, covered in flavoured paste is set in the right spot as a trap for a big barbel looking for her breakfast or supper. Tony uses Flourocarbon, Dacron or Snakebite hook links, carefully choosing the right link for the right swim. I must say that braided hook lengths have certainly upped my success rate with barbel.

Legering near bank - close downstream.

© Clare Yates

Barbel often hug the river bed next to banks and undercuts, here the current speed is slowed by friction. Also, the bank offers cover (fringing reedy vegetation, low-level bushes, crowfoot beds, tree root masses, boulders, deadwood snags, etc), providing vital security for wary fish. This technique is great for clear-watered rivers in summer when a stealthy walk with a wide-brimmed hat and polaroids can pin point a pod of barbel. The method involves fishing a short distance downstream, with a light leger placed close in under the near bank, either with the rod in rests or held to allow touch legering. A drilled bullet weight rolls nicely in under the bank. Bites can vary from tingles on the line to rod-wrenching sail-aways. Natural baits are worth a go. This method, used to great effect by Fred Crouch (see Fred's excellent 'Understanding barbel') suits the cane rod plus centre pin enthusiast. Hemp and free offerings can be accurately introduced with stealthy use of a bait-dropper. It is essential to sit back very quietly and give resident fish time to settle down and feed confidently. Barbel can be caught from 'under your feet' provided that they have not been alerted to danger. The bank provides you with excellent cover but vibrations must be kept to a minimum to avoid scaring the fish.

Weed bombing

Andy Orme has written of his outstanding middle Avon and lower Stour barbel catches, noting that in summer when barbel hide under crowfoot beds it is sometimes worth lobbing a heavy bomb into gaps in the weed and then pulling the line gently to check that you have hit bottom. This is critical as sitting with your hook link tangled up in half a hundredweight of weed is not a forerunner of success. An alternative to bombing through the weed is to swing a bait downstream and across on a tight line, letting the current take the rig in under the edge of a weed bed. In this way shy barbel can be encouraged to bite whilst you remain shielded from view by the weeds. This is a good example of working with the river to help you catch fish, rather than struggling against the prevailing conditions. Where conditions and rules permit, stealthy wading and dropping baits on light tackle into holes in the weed is a good summer tactic. Another important ploy for weedy barbel swims is to forget about trying to pull a fish upstream through the weed towards your hand or net. Don't bother; work your way down below the barbel and play it downstream through the weed - this is easy by comparison. This advice is especially important if you are to avoid over-straining a prized bamboo rod.

Far bank feeder fishing

When barbel are shoaled up along the far bank or in a deep glide or pool well away from your own bank, you are forced to fish at long-range. This will usually entail using a quiver tip rod, held high in rests to keep the line out of the water, coupled with a swim feeder rig cast across and downstream allowing the building up of a swim well away from you with regular introductions of hemp, corn, maggots/casters, etc. This approach can be combined with observation on medium-sized clear water rivers like the Hampshire Avon. For instance, Pete Reading often favours swim-feedered hemp and casters to build up the barbel's confidence, followed by four casters superglued to a fine hair rig and presented on a braided trace. Close observation allows Pete to judge when to present a bait - when the barbel are well and truly on the feed - and not before.

The Severn in summer responds to similar tactics except that you often can't see the fish and you can afford to use a simpler rig. Well known Severn matchman Barry Cooper has had 100lb bags of barbel on block end feeder rigs with 6lb Maxima hook links; once again hemp and caster is the deadly combination. Barry keeps the feed going in for some time before expecting his first fish, once he has a barbel shoal feeding well, he confidently expects to catch fish one after the other. I seldom have this degree of confidence!

In powerful rivers like the Severn, Trent or lower Wye, especially during winter, you will need stout gear and a heavy feeder to fish the far bank. Archie Braddock's book (Fantastic feeder fishing) describes this method in detail. Archie made his feeders from chunks of aluminium tubing weighted down with large lead strips. Lighter rigs are feasible in summer, especially on smaller rivers. Fishing at range means that barbel are less likely to see or hear you but they will need to get over the splash of the feeder before they gain confidence to feed. Where angling pressure isn't too high barbel learn to search for food as soon as the feeder arrives and will even tackle it 'on the drop' if really feeding well. This is where the 'rubber band rig', securing the hook link tight to the feeder came from.

As warm spates subside and the river still carries some colour (strong tea/brown ale), feeder fishing with hemp / maggots or hemp / meat / corn is a very telling method. In fast currents cage feeders offer less resistance to the flow, see Roger Miller's book for details on recommended tangle-free rigs. When the river is full of flotsam - after a weed cut or autumn spate, dip your rod tip below the surface and touch leger - this works well and can salvage an otherwise hopeless situation.

Downstream balanced leger

By ground baiting with, for example, a Des Taylor recommended mix of Van Den Eynde River Ace, brown bread crumb and grilled hemp in equal quantities (plus a lacing of hook baits) you can produce a 'smell lane' through a swim and beyond, attracting barbel from well down stream. Mix the groundbait balls very stiffly so that they break down slowly and give the barbel time to move into the feeding area. Give the fish a chance to settle down before fishing.

Fishing 20-30 metres down stream and across you can swing a leger into the ground baited area so that it just holds bottom. Use a clip swivel so that you can change weights easily, critically balancing your rig which will then have minimal resistance to a shy barbel mouthing the bait. Baits can be maggot, bread flake, meat, corn, pastes, etc. If you quietly build up a swim, choosing an area where bank walkers won't spook the fish, you can entice a shoal of confidently feeding barbel to within comfortable fishing range. Stick to relatively open glides and pools as heavy weed growth makes it very difficult to play fish back upstream.

Light-legering upstream.

Barbel often move onto pool tails and into open glides in late evening to forage for food in shallow areas where they do not generally feel safe during the day. As mentioned above, it can be very difficult to play and land fish by attempting to pull them upstream through the weed but much easier to guide them downstream towards you in between the weed beds. An upstream approach is, therefore, sound and can allow the use of relatively light tackle in weedy swims.

By casting a leger upstream and keeping the rod tip high so as to minimise the amount of line underwater, drag is kept down and lighter rigs can be used. A long rod (12 foot plus) helps with presentation, I have a Harrison 15 foot stepped up carbon float rod which is perfect for this approach. Bites will often be 'drop-backs' and care is needed to distinguish between down stream drifting of the leger and real bites. Striking too frequently at false alarms may spook fish. A link leger set-up allows adding or subtracting shot to suit varying conditions so that you can get the balance just right. Natural baits are worth a go with this method. When applied carefully, this approach can be very deadly for shy fish, as you are downstream of them they are unlikely to see you.

John Ginifer, amongst others, has used the approach to great effect for Thames barbel (see Peter Wheat's 'The fighting barbel'). Whilst gaining experience with this technique John noticed that getting barbel bites seemed to be linked to accurate bait placement within a swim. This suggests that barbel may have been using particular feeding areas or routes - this idea has since been confirmed by the intensive studies of Stuart Morgan and Guy Robb ('ghosting' - see below). John also noticed that when dace bites started to fall away, the chances of catching barbel increased - perhaps shoaling dace avoid foraging barbel for fear of being eaten. John Bickerdyke had similar thoughts back in 1888. Make no mistake about it - barbel will happily snaffle a small fish when they get the chance.

Remember that a length of fine lead wire wound around the hook shank can be a good substitute for a conventional leger rig. You can easily vary the weight of the hook to suit various swims. The bulky hook shank is hidden within the bait (usually meat or paste) and the weighted 'free-lined' rig is then used to trundle through glides and pools. Trefor West has used this ruse to fool many a Bristol Avon barbel - matching the drift of the bait close to the river bed with the surrounding current speed often fools fish which are wary of tethered baits (see 'trundling' - below).

Upstream balanced feeder

An upstream-cast feeder which is weighted so as to just hold bottom is a deadly rig. A bow of line is allowed to form so that you are hardly in direct contact with the terminal tackle. Archie Braddock pioneered this method on the Trent. Upon taking the bait the fish feels virtually no resistance and, as it turns downstream, the feeder follows. A bite registered on a quiver tip is a simple drop back and the response need only be a steady retrieve until contact is made with the fish. Archie Braddock (reading list) explains the subtle aspects of this really telling method - in the hands of an expert, like him, virtually no bites are missed.

Free lining

The ultimately sensitive approach to upstream legering is to free line a large bait such as a ball of spicy paste, a lob worm, cockle, prawn or chunk of luncheon meat. The bait will drop to the bottom in all but the fastest of flows. Where barbel are wary of ordinary-sized cubes of meat, a very large (quarter of a tin!) bait can provoke a savage response, especially when allowed to drift through the swim on weightless tackle.

When cast upstream between crowfoot beds or into the head of a pool, the line can be recovered carefully as the bait bumps its way back towards you whilst you touch leger for bites. This is a telling method if combined with quiet wading to reach difficult swims. Even the most gentle of takes are detectable and played-out fish can be released whilst still in the water without even having to net them. Barbless hooks make catch-and-release much easier but remember to make sure that your barbel are fully able to swim away strongly before you let them go.

Trundling

Barbel may find food either buried in the river bed or drifting past them in the current. When occupying a swim with a rapid current and clean bed, barbel do not expect to see relatively light food offerings tethered static on the gravel......they should be drifting along close to the bed at a similar rate to the surrounding current. Natural baits are well worth a go when trundling. Ray Walton has perfected the presentation of meaty baits in this way, using small adjustments in leger weight (moulded Plasticine/tungsten putty or swan shot) and allowing the bait to move progressively through each swim. Howard Maddocks trundled four halves of Campbells Meat Balls to catch his 1998 16lb 3oz River Severn barbel - a record holding fish at that time.

Trundling is, then, the legering equivalent of trotting a float-fished bait - matching the current speed to the motion of the bait and presenting it at barbel nose level. By keeping low and moving stealthily a lot of water can be covered. On heavily fished waters where most anglers stick to the 'chuck it out and sit in hope' philosophy, this approach will be much more successful. The Royalty fishery on the Avon and Throop on the Stour are two cases in point.

Float fishing - long-trotting

Long trotting on the lower Trent was traditionally practised using very large floats supporting an ounce or more of lead! Such rigs allow slow searching of the bed in deep swirling waters. This point is worth remembering - you may need to use a three or four swan shot float on powerful rivers to ensure a smoothly moving bait. Give a small natural bait a swim through every so often - you may be surprised at the result.

Trotting provides the perfect method for the long light rod, balsa on crow quill float and centre pin reel. The pioneering F.W.K. Wallis used this technique to great effect on the Hampshire Avon Royalty fishery, many superb barbel falling to his cane Wallis Wizard float rod. Today, sound, rebuilt originals or brand new cane rods are in great demand and the work of modern craftsmen such as Edward Barder is well worth waiting for. There are also, of course, many superb carbon trotting rods which have the necessary backbone to deal with hard-fighting barbel. Davis Tackle in Christchurch do a good one based on a high quality Harrison blank. Andy Orme's SEER rod company build some nice ones too. A quality 'pin will give line at precisely the speed dictated by the current and gentle thumb pressure on the rim allows the line to be held back - sweeping the bait over snags or allowing it to waver enticingly in the current. Nice fishing.

In the hands of an expert, trotting is a potent method for taking barbel occupying runs between crowfoot beds, long gravel-bedded glides, pools and scour holes. Regular handfuls of hook bait with hemp can build up a swim so that a barbel shoal is encouraged to move in and feed actively, even in broad daylight. Take a big bucket of bait though - you need to keep the food going in regularly to encourage fish to feed. Bill Leavesley described the method to perfection in Angling Times August 5th 1998. Fishing the Severn at 'Barbel Alley' just downstream of Bewdley, Bill kept the feed going in before each cast with a small handful of hemp, caster and diced luncheon meat. Using three pound Maxima straight through to a 14 or 12 forged hook with bulked AAA shot below a big Avon, Chubber or Topper, Bill fished from a punt to direct his trotted float through a metre deep swim. By holding the float back momentarily next to big boulders and weed beds the barbel are given time to nip out from cover and snaffle the hook bait. In 1996 Bill caught caught barbel of 10lb 2oz and 10lb 6oz on consecutive casts on a single grain of trotted hemp on a 14 hook. You don't need a big bait to catch actively feeding big barbel. Just imagine how fast their reflexes are and how good their eyesight is to pick up these tiny baits in a fast current.

Laying-on in slacks.

© MGN Ltd

Where barbel are lying up in bank side slacks or out of the main force of the current in creases, behind large boulders, tree snags or dense weed beds, food will naturally drop out of the flow and sit on the river bed. Here, a static bait is likely to be accepted with little suspicion, provided that your rig is sound and you haven't scared the fish in your approach. An over-depth float with a single swan shot or small nugget of tungsten putty on the bed can be carefully set so as to provide very sensitive bite-detection. It's also a lot of fun watching a float. At dusk a Beta light on the float or a carefully angled torch allows the method to be used well into the twilight. A long, limber, rod, lightish line and a steady hand make this a superb summer evening method. Naturals like worm, cockle, mussel and prawn are well worth a go - try something different.

Stret-pegging

This method, recently re-popularised by John Wilson (Catch Barbel), is also an over-depth float fishing method but here the bait is fished immediately downstream in a deep near-bank run and the float is dragged under by the flow when the bait is taken. The float is attached top and bottom with silicone tubing and set at perhaps twice the water depth. A light leger sits on the bottom and a downstream bow in the line is allowed to develop back up to the float which lies flat on the surface. The line from rod tip to float is kept out of the water, by lifting the rod tip occasionally the bait can be edged downstream - the original trundling approach. A fish taking the bait dislodges the leger downstream, meeting minimal resistance, and the float shoots under - great! Baits can be accurately placed in scoops on the bed, next to snags, etc and shy barbel encouraged to feed very close to where you are sitting. As usual, a sound knowledge of the water, stealth and fish spotting abilities are essential for success.

Float fishing minnows....and spinning for barbel?

Way back in 1932 Patrick Chalmers wrote of catching Thames barbel on minnows by trotting a float over the tail of mill pools. In Peter Wheat's book, the legendary Peter Stone described how, as a teenager, he too deliberately caught Thames barbel from the gravelly tail of a large bridge pool on trotted minnow fished under a small cork. I have seen barbel on the Wye efficiently arcing through the depths of a pool, chasing minnow shoals up onto gravel shallows before engulfing their prey. Tim Pryke tells me that Wye barbel often take dead minnows with gusto, but are difficult to hook. He has used them in tandem with a small feeder - the feeder attracts a shoal of minnows, the minnows attract a barbel, the minnow bait catches the barbel. This sequence proved to work really well apart from the hooking the barbel bit. Tim wonders whether the ferocity of the bites and difficulty in making any connection is linked to the barbel having to attack at speed to suck up its prey. Barbel do, of course, lack the jaw teeth normally associated with a predatory fish and may make up for this in this way. I wonder if a minnow tethered to a feeder rig is held back from being sucked in as the barbel dashes by, leading to missed takes? Perhaps using a longer trace or a popped-up minnow would help overcome this problem.

Minnows forming breeding shoals on gravel shallows in the early summer represent a high protein food source for barbel. Whilst chasing each other during courtship the brightly coloured males and fat, slow-moving females bulging with eggs may be especially vulnerable. Perhaps fish-eating in spring and early summer forms part of a regular annual feeding cycle for barbel preparing themselves for the rigours of spawning and subsequently regaining condition whilst 'cleaning up' on the gravel shallows. William Yarrell, (1859 - A History of British Fishes) noted that anglers spinning small deadbaits for large Thames trout sometimes caught barbel. Peter Wheat (Fishing as we find it) mentioned that, in Germany, spinning for barbel with thin metal spoons is quite common with fish up to 12 - 14 pounds taken. Interesting.

Maybe the very big barbel caught by anglers spinning for spring salmon on the Hampshire Avon during the coarse fish close season were fish deliberately hunting minnows on the shallows. A brightly coloured 'Devon minnow' may be a fair representation of a male minnow in nuptial colours. Examples of barbel caught in this way include a 14 pounder at Burgate, off the front lawn of The Game Conservancy Trust, weighed on the post room scales and returned alive, Roy Beddington's 16lb 4oz monster, hooked fairly on a spun dace, a 16lb 1oz fish for Charles Cassey at Ibsley and a 17lb 8oz fish at Avon Tyrell by Lady Rothes. These are by no means the only mega-barbel to come out of the Avon on spun natural baits and lures - several very big fish have come out of the lowermost fishery - The Royalty. A key point to realise is that, during all the years that spring salmon anglers took occasional massive Avon barbel - way above the then record of 14lb 6oz, none of these monsters was caught by conventional barbel fishermen. Despite the fact that much of the Avon was exclusively salmon fishing water at that time, there was still a fair bit of barbel fishing done. Maybe spinning really could be selective for Barbus maximus. As has been mooted by barbel anglers in the past, a slowly spun artificial minnow or similar lure could be the key to catching wary early season specimen barbel today.

Ghosting

Stuart Morgan and Guy Robb have developed a deadly combination of studies of weather and cycles of the moon with close observation of barbel swims and patrol routes (see John Baker's book). They have watched barbel move predictably from safe daytime lies deep in cover to late evening shallower feeding areas. However, the key added element which their patient observations have revealed is that barbel use precise routes to get from one place to another - often following the deepest (and presumably safest) scrapes and channels available. After a suitable phase of pre-baiting, a tempting morsel (eg a John Baker Barbel Search 4 flavoured paste bait) is cast accurately onto the well-worn route so as to intercept a fish cruising towards a natural evening feeding session - brilliant and effective. Once again, long hours of patient observation lead to success; both Stuart and Guy have caught 17 pound barbel from differing stretches of the Great Ouse with this sort of approach. It is worth noting that Peter Wheat, writing in the 1960s, described the regular routes taken by barbel shoals in given swims and used by one observant angler to take three consecutive ten pounders on cheese from the Royalty fishery's Railway pool under low-flow conditions.

More recently Martin Hooper has been very successful on the Hants Avon and Dorset Stour, using long periods of 'polaroiding'- stealthily walking the bank observing fish and then fishing whenever possible in clear water so as to be able to target big barbel. Martin has deliberately pulled his bait away from double figure fish when an even larger specimen is around..... nerves of steel!

Fly fishing

Coarse fish such as dace and chub are well known to be catchable on dry flies. Some folk chase pike and perch with big streamer flies purposefully and both species get caught on a range of nymphs and lures by reservoir trout fishermen. Catching barbel on deeply-fished nymphs should not seem strange, after all, they naturally eat plenty of invertebrates. Despite this, as far as I know, few anglers have tried deliberately fly-rodding for barbel in the UK. Peter Wheat (Fishing as we find it) does give a few examples including several barbel taken on nymphs and other flies from the Kennet, Upper Thames and Swale. Recently, John Bailey has had some success on the middle Wye catching quite a few barbel on gold-headed nymphs. Tim Pryke has experimented along the same stretch of river and caught several barbel by trundling an Oliver Edwards 'peeping caddis' larva imitation on standard barbel trundling tackle. I'm told that, further south in Europe, fly-caught coarse fish, including barbel are not unusual - the Germans and Czechs are quite adept at it. Czechs use heavily weighted nymphs to fish for grayling and there is quite a bit of scope for experimentation here, I reckon. A barbel hooked on nymphing fly tackle would be a force to be reckoned with. Where river conditions allow a delicate approach with visible fish this could prove to be whole new ball game. Why not give it a go, John Wilson's carp catching on fly gear is catching on in popularity, could barbel be next?

Barbel tackle

Rods

© MGN Ltd

Cane, glass and carbon rods all have their fans - I have used all three from time to time and like them all for their various properties.

There is something about bamboo rods which makes them nice to use - natural materials and quality construction :

"using rods made from a weird kind of grass that grows in China seems somehow appropriate"

John Gierach Trout Bum.

For cane fanciers I can recommend Edward Barder's : Barbus maximus (marks I and II) and Merlin, Chapman Brothers Fred J. Taylor Roach, and 500 (Avon), B. James Avocet and Kennet Perfection and Allcocks Wallis Wizard. I'm sure there are many other good ones that I haven't had a chance to get my paws on. Amongst older rods, in weedy swims and heavy water the Roach rod, Wizard and Kennet Perfection are under-gunned and you may be better off with an early whole cane butt James Avocet. Finding a good example of a 40 year old rod is, however, no easy matter - be very careful in the minefield which is the second hand cane rod market!

It is still possible to pick up cheap, old, but perfectly serviceable cane rods if you keep looking and aren't in a race. Buying unseen through 2nd hand adverts in the angling weeklies or on the internet is asking for trouble - I speak from experience. Also, I feel I must mention that there are worries about some 'restored' old cane rods which are not what they purport to be - be careful. Imagine the disappointment of taking ages to track down the rod of your dreams, finely finished with many coats of varnish, only to find that it is a lash-up comprised of various sections from semi-knackered rods. Not all cane rod outlets are like this, of course, many are probably absolutely fine. Take advice from the experts. For those of you who visit the Hampshire Avon, it's well worth dropping in on John Searl's shop in Ringwood - John always has some genuine and fairly-priced cane rods on sale. Up in the Midlands, Steve Middleton (Traditional Angling) also often gets hold of some good gear. In south Wales, Victor Bonutto is constantly scanning for sound second hand classic fishing tackle and he is always at the CLA Game Fair with his immaculate stall crammed with fair-priced goodies.

I include the following details of Edward Barder's rods as I know they are of excellent quality. I have no axe to grind here, when I buy a Barder rod it will cost me full price.

The Edward Barder Rod Co.
Makers of the finest split cane rods.

The Chris Yates MKII Barbus Maximus 11' 2-piece Barbel rod.

Now in its twelfth year of production, the Barbus Maximus has become the quintessential split cane barbel rod. Rated for 6~8 lb line, its through action embodies the best qualities of fine split cane, the most tactile of rod building materials: a sensitive yet durable tip, smooth, progressive power, good balance and enough backbone to handle the largest barbel.

The rod is built to peerless standards of design and attention to detail. We make every part of the rod from scratch in our workshop (apart from the rings and rubber button). The blank is made from hand-tempered seasoned Tonkin bamboo, the handle fittings and ferrules from nickel silver, and the whippings are finest silk. Our lustrous hand-applied varnish finish is genuinely flawless and has no equal.

For more information about the Barbus Maximus and our other rods, please telephone, write or e-mail. A catalogue will be sent gratis, on request, or visit our web site. Visits to our workshop are strictly by appointment.

The Edward Barder Rod Co
Ham Mill, London Road, Newbury,
Berkshire, RH14 2BU
Telephone/Fax 01635 552916
E-mail: edward@barder-rod.co.uk

www.barder-rod.co.uk

Edward kindly wrote the following section for those considering the purchase of a bamboo rod:

Split cane rods for the barbel angler

Let's face it, these days virtually all fishing rods are made from carbon fibre, so it's no wonder that the continued devotion some of us show for split cane is questioned. In his splendid book, 'In The Ring Of The Rise', Vincent Marinaro put his finger on it nicely when he noted that:

'Bamboo, being a natural product, like flesh and blood, can establish a greater affinity with its owner than any other material. There can be a powerful personal bond between them, an identification that lets the caster feel that the rod is an extension of his own personality. It goes beyond mere pride of ownership.'

It is doubtful whether any angler would not cast an appreciative eye over an old cane rod hanging above the mantelpiece in a riverside pub. A carbon fibre job in its place would point towards the publican's lack of taste.

Aesthetics aside though, we must ask ourselves whether or not split cane is really worth fishing with, considering that one hundred pounds or so will buy us a thoroughly functional, low maintenance carbon fibre barbel rod. To qualify the answer to this question, we should bear in mind that until about forty years ago, all the best rods were made from bamboo, and people went fishing quite happily. They caught plenty of whoppers too, but with the advent of reliable 'plastic' rods, anglers were able to develop techniques that the limitations of bamboo had largely ruled out.

A day spent trotting heavy float tackle along the far bank of a big river using a carbon fourteen footer is perfectly feasible. Half an hour of the same with a bamboo equivalent would be virtually impossible. Likewise, regularly casting a baiting engine the size of a small child to the head of a barbel swim on the tidal Trent would almost immediately knacker your favourite MK IV carp rod. A carbon 'feeder' rod though, if it had any character, would be urging you to cast into the next valley, shrugging off the consequences without so much as a creak. Of course, swims far from the bank were float-fished in split cane's golden age, and a prodigious quantity of bait was often thrown in. From a punt!

Carbon fibre won the strength-to-weight ratio competition, but, where appropriate, a really fine cane rod can be the sweetest handling, most responsive and tactile tool for barbeling with. That dense bundle of bamboo fibres really does transmit to the hand what is happening along the line, and it does fight back against being bent with life and vigour. Well made and in good order, such rods are reliable too, not just arcane relics for the tweed pyjamas and worsted undergarments fraternity.

So, for all but the most extreme forms of tackle manipulation, we may use cane rods without the forearms of Hercules, and without detracting one iota from our chances of catching a fish. But, with a century of cane rod production to choose from, both vintage and modern, which makers should we favour, which particular model would best suit our purposes? Important questions these, when faced with a probable outlay of several hundred pounds and the overriding requirement for a good rod that won't snap like a carrot on the first fish you hook with it.

Split cane rods are currently being made by a newt's handful of small specialist firms. This should be good news for today's cane enthusiast. These makers have the benefit of reference to vintage rods, the availability of superior glues, varnishes and metals to work with. Their market is small, so they are not forced into mass production techniques to cut corners. Ideally, their rod designs will be arrived at as a result of their own angling experiences. Nowadays, there is no reason to settle for less, and no excuses for new rods that are not an improvement on the vintage models. By making thoughtful enquiries, it should be perfectly possible to satisfy yourself that the new cane rod you buy will be a real treasure.

Bear in mind though, that to make a cane barbel rod to the highest possible standard, a skilled professional may put in up to sixty hours hard work. It doesn't take a genius to work out that even the heftiest price tag reflects a meagre hourly rate of pay. In reality, you are getting a bargain. Unlike in America and Japan, where the fine cane rod is revered enough to justify the publication of magazines devoted to them, we British often have a detrimentally mean attitude. For instance, without flinching, we buy mass produced video cameras that will be obsolete in no time, for the asking price of a new cane rod that may still be fishable a hundred years from now. People grumble and balk, lack patience and deny the existence of the perfectly usable credit cards fighting to get out of their plump wallets. They shouldn't, or the craft will fade away and, as ever, people will shake their heads and mourn the absence of dear old so-and-so the rod builder, who is now earning a relative fortune as a seasonal fruit picker in Herefordshire. If this doesn't wash with you, happy citizen of currently the fourth largest economy in the world, perhaps Hilaire Belloc's *Lord Finchley* should have the last word:

> *"It is the business of the wealthy man
> To give employment to the artisan."*

And so we arrive at the second half of our little chat. Yes, you there, with the spats and the monocle, this is very much your bag, so pay attention; handy hints on vintage cane rods around the next bend. But firstly, let's dispense with a myth or two.

Old split cane rods, say their fans, are so nice because they're hand-made. How sweet, and how mistaken. Remember that these rods were the norm in their day, produced by often very large firms in great numbers. They were mostly made to a price and although bamboo was the raw material, machines played a very large part in their construction. This does not mean that the rods were all bad. If the machinery was good and the operators skilled, the results were perfectly all right. Happily, bamboo's innate qualities are still present in good production rods, and their looks are pretty consistently what we have come to expect. Of the better known firms who produced rods still likely to be around now, only Olivers of Knebworth made genuinely hand-built rods. Although the early B James production was based on much hand building, their more common later rods were really high-grade production jobs. Even the whippings were machine-tied and doped in place. Damned crafty if you ask me. None of this is meant scornfully. As ever, one gets what one pays for, which brings us to the second myth, which concerns relative prices. For example:

'*Cor blimey glubnor, how much? I remember going into old Frank Maggot's shop at Gentle Corner and buying my first B James MK IV for ten guineas back in 1958. Aren't they dear now!*' '*Got any size ten schwibbles?*'

How could one ever tire of such penetrating observations, when they give one the opportunity to graciously remind Sir that in 1958, the average weekly wage was three shillings and sixpence, and that the national diet comprised largely of dubbin, cups of tea, cardboard and turnips. Now that the average wage is quite a bit higher, and life expectancy for men is more than twenty-five years, today's prices seem quite reasonable.

It would not serve our purposes here to dig up the more obscure makers of the past, or the countless shop-branded rods built by the trade. This Byzantine aspect of vintage rod buying is very interesting and worthy, when one has largely lost interest in life, but for now we will concern ourselves with makes we are most likely to encounter as we ferret about in the fusty crevices and dank corners of the tackle trade. These include:

Hardy's of Alnwick, Foster Bros. of Ashbourne and Sharpe's of Aberdeen. Allcocks, Milwards, Lee, Aspindale, Martin James and Edgar Sealey were all from Redditch. In London and the Home Counties were B.James & Son, Cliff Constable, Davenport and Fordham, R.Chapman & Co, Bob (*The Captain*) Southwell, Eggington, F.T.Williams, J.B.Walker, Ogden Smiths, T.H.Sowerbutts, Homer's, Young's and Oliver's.

Primed with all this information, you are already a connoisseur and very nearly an expert. All that remains is to go out and buy wisely. If you're the sort of gent who considers himself the practical type, and know which end of the hammer to hold when banging in a screw, carry on. If, on the other hand, you are very brainy at maths but have trouble doing up your shoelaces, look away now.

Assuming that they urged you towards a cane rod in the first place, you should put your emotions away for a while. This is the time to summon up the healthy common sense that saved you, in the nick of time, from buying that high mileage Ford Anglia at the car auction last autumn. You're a barbel angler after all, so you know what you want from a rod. For trotting, the weight and balance should be manageable, the length appropriate, and the rings spaced close enough. The action should be forgiving, but not too sloppy. The legering rod you need will have a sensitive tip, though not so fine that it will collapse when casting a heavy weight into a flooded river. It should have a progressive action, with plenty of power in the lower third. Neither rod should be anything less than mechanically sound and rods which bend too much in one place or display any other eccentricities are of no use to you. Above all, the rods you use, cane or otherwise, should properly suit the water you fish and the size of barbel you hope to catch. There follows a typical rod-buying scenario:

In his almost impenetrable foreign accent, the charming vendor suggests that you may like the Kennet Perfection by B.James & Son. It has a nice heft to it and is named after a grand barbel river. You put a line through its rings and direct your friend to hold on and make like a fish. You soon realise that this example would be fine for dace, but not much use against the fellows you're after. Another rod of the same name is handed to you; this time from Oliver's of Knebworth. The tapers of this one produce a different action altogether. It too feels nice in the hand, but has enough power to stop your fish-impersonating chum from reaching the end of the car park. It's tempting, but on close inspection, you see that it has suffered rather from neglect and hard use. The ferrules are badly worn, the rings are grooved and the varnish is tatty. At two hundred and fifty pounds, with a similar sum needed for a professional restoration, it's looking like a borderline case.

From another bag is drawn an Avocet, also by B.James. You've heard of this one. Its a good length at eleven and quarter feet and handy in three sections. This example isn't too top-heavy, and your companion holding the line, in danger of losing his identity and claiming to be a 'mid-double', lets you feel the sensitive yet strong tip curve smoothly down to the mid-section. Then he tries to get behind your Humber Super Snipe and you use the power in the whole cane butt to turn him. He's beaten, and by now quite mad, but you've proved that the rod would serve you well.

With its rings to one side, you sight down it and see that it hasn't gone the way of the banana. The ferrules a nice 'honeymoon' fit and the rings, whippings and varnish are sound. The caramel-coloured cane joints show no open seams at the corners, the ferrule stoppers are there, along with the maker's rod bag, and the cork handle isn't soggy. You ponder it over a can of Tizer, decide you want it and ask 'how much?' 'Six hundred of your English pounds', you are told firmly.

You can't help yourself and blurt out 'Get knotted Major! That's a fortnight's wages. Who do you think I am? Aristotle Onassis!'

Now you know what you are looking for, but you'll have to go out and get a proper job so that you can afford it. Still keeping the practical you to the fore for a moment, bear the following in mind: bargains may still turn up in tackle, antique and junk shops, at auctions, in the small ads of diverse publications and within the internet. Do not under any circumstances buy a second hand cane rod that you have not inspected thoroughly. A reputable dealer will send you a rod on approval if you cannot visit. Some security may be required, although I doubt to the extent of your mum being held temporarily hostage, and you will have to pay the carriage charge. Dealers may well ask premium prices and good for them. Remember that they have money tied up in stock, offer a choice, have rent and rates to pay, and usually fourteen or fifteen children and a sick goat to feed.

Before we wave our silk hankies in fond farewell to vintage cane, don't forget that elderly rods cannot be returned to their now extinct makers for repairs or servicing. A knackered old rod is not worth a bean, and the subtle bargains and restoration projects are best left to the handful of people who can make sense of them. Your friends may smile fondly at your quaint old twelve footer by Cornelius Stickleback & Son of Tooting, but no barbel will like you for the hook and a yard of line you leave it with, thanks to the rod's abrasively grooved rings.

Thanks Edward - good advice.

A good bamboo rod is very nice to use, being a natural material and a good one has a steely, fish-taming quality which is reassuring and reliable. Cane rods are, however, necessarily expensive and prone to damage in car doors, under waders and anywhere near young children and fishing dogs. Treated with care, a good cane rod will last many a season.

A few useful tips on cane (based on Edward Barder's wide experience) are:
- Don't cast leads or use lines heavier than the rod was designed for. Multiply the test curve by about 5 to get the safe breaking strain of line to use on a sound, through action, cane rod.
- When playing barbel after barbel (let's be optimistic) occasionally

turn the rod over to even out tensions - this will help to avoid 'sets' (bends) in the long-term.

- When landing a fish try not to bend the tip over too tightly - use a long-handled net to keep your distance. This helps to reduce the chance of stressing or breaking tips.

- When wandering along the bank, carry the rod handle-first, this also reduces the chance of busting the tip.

- When you get snagged pull straight on the line for a break - not through the rod.

- When the ferrules seem to get stuck, use a couple of pieces of cycle inner tube (tucked into your bag for the purpose) to get a good grip. Many 'stuck ferrules' are actually slippery hands! Don't twist rod sections when pulling ferrules apart - pull them straight. Twisting cane can split the sections apart.

- Don't leave a cane rod stuffed in a corner in a wet rod bag. Dry off rods after use and hang them up straight (vertically, with tips pointing up) in a loosely-tied bag. If leaving rods for a long time move the sections every so often or store them on a flat shelf.

- If you get sticky ferrules wipe them over lightly with a cloth dipped in white spirit and then polish them up on the curtains, table cloth or shirt cuff when the wife isn't looking. Don't use Meths or abrasives on ferrules - you will soon spoil the finish on your rod and you may loosen the ferrules.

- If you buy a rod with loose ferrules, take it to an expert who may be able to sort it out without the substantial cost of ferrule renewal. Giving the female a squeeze (great work if you can get it) is not recommended in this context. A bit of soap on the male ferrule can, however, add a season or two to a worn joint.

The use of cane isn't just an old fart's affliction - they really do make excellent rods.

Old fibreglass rods, for instance, by Hardy or Bruce & Walker - Avons, barbel and carp models have very nice, soft actions and are capable of taming the biggest of barbel in open water swims. Snag fishing is another matter, here carbon comes into its own. This sort of strong arm stuff isn't my cup of tea but each to their own. Glass rods have their detractors because of their softness but I like them - especially the Hardy brown glass rods which seem virtually indestructible (candle waxing the ferrules makes then last longer). Buying these types of rod second hand is usually pretty trouble-free.

For the carbon fibre man I strongly recommend rods built on Harrison blanks (www.harrisonrods.co.uk). Harrisons only supply trade outlets, the web site gives details of your local dealer. The Quorum and Triptych models are both very good specialist barbel rods, the Quorum being a stiffer blank than the Triptych. Steve Harrison also makes a superb 15 foot stepped-up float rod which is set to become my favourite summer river rod. The blanks for many specialist barbel rods are manufactured by Harrisons but branded under a variety of names. Other companies such as Hardy, Drennan, Bruce & Walker, Normark, Daiwa, Shimano, Giant, Fox, and Free Spirit also market good quality carbon rods but be careful - actions vary widely, ideally, try get hold of one and fish with it before you buy. Seer rods (www.seer-rods.co.uk) and Graham Phillips rods are used by many and have good reputations. Bruce & Walker Hexagraphs (hexagonal carbon jobs) have serious backbone and are light and crisp, they are relatively expensive but have their devotees.

Reels - Centre pins

For trotting, old Aerial match reels are excellent and Speedias, Trudex, Rapidex, etc do a good job too. Trotting reels need light drums with low inertia. Go for one with little or no wobble between the centre pin and the spool. For legering, heavier, wide spooled Aerials or good quality modern copies are very nice. Any 'pins made by J.W. Youngs are likely to be sound. For the centre-pinners out there who wish to explore the far bank, try to learn how to 'Wallis' cast - the line whizzing off the fast-revolving drum until gently braked with the little finger. Or, in my case, the line springing off the spool with alarming speed to form a tightly plaited nylon mosquito screen. Maybe some more practice would help. All cane and centre-pin users must, of course, wear faded old cord trousers with the backside hanging out of them, tweedy jacket and floppy hat. A pipe also helps.

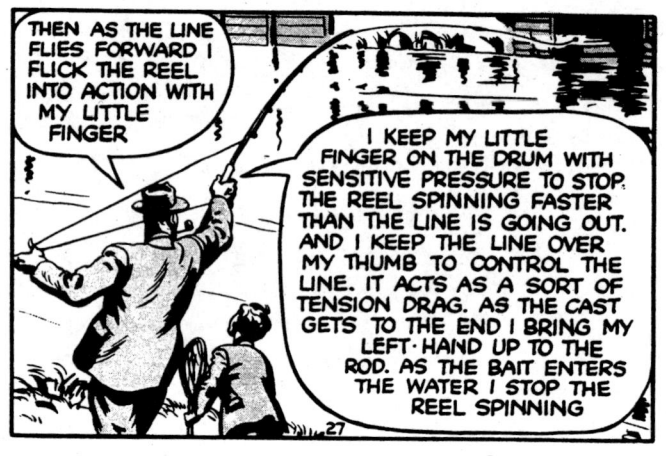

> THEN AS THE LINE FLIES FORWARD I FLICK THE REEL INTO ACTION WITH MY LITTLE FINGER
>
> I KEEP MY LITTLE FINGER ON THE DRUM WITH SENSITIVE PRESSURE TO STOP THE REEL SPINNING FASTER THAN THE LINE IS GOING OUT. AND I KEEP THE LINE OVER MY THUMB TO CONTROL THE LINE. IT ACTS AS A SORT OF TENSION DRAG. AS THE CAST GETS TO THE END I BRING MY LEFT·HAND UP TO THE ROD. AS THE BAIT ENTERS THE WATER I STOP THE REEL SPINNING

© MGN Ltd

Chris Yates when fishing at Breamore Mill on the Hampshire Avon a few seasons ago cocked up a Wallis cast, sorted the resulting 'bird's nest' for a couple of minutes, started to retrieve his luncheon meat and fastened firmly into a 12 pound-plus barbel.....only Chris could do that.

Fixed spools

I have caught most of my barbel on old Mitchell 410s and Cardinal 55s. These days, Shimano make such good reels that it hardly seems worth mentioning the competition. I'm sure, however, that most of the other major manufacturers also make very reliable and sound reels. It's a bit like family cars - virtually all of them are amazingly good these days. In the end, most people fish with what they enjoy using the best. A reliable clutch and line roller are really handy when the bertie of your dreams decides that 30 yards downstream looks a better bet than inside your landing net.

Hooks

I use barbless hooks of various makes and have had few problems. Barbel are very powerful and so demand sturdy hooks - keep them within reason size-wise, it makes a difference to the welfare of the fish.

Line

I use Maxima nylon and a variety of hook length materials, depending on circumstances. I have caught double figure barbel from the Hants Avon, Dorset Stour, Wye and Bristol Avon on 6lb Maxima and find it very reliable with a useful degree of stretch when the breeze whistles across a taut line. Anglers liking tougher lines may go for Berkeley XT or Silver Thread, both developed for heavy duty work. Braided mainlines are useful under extreme conditions but nylon seems to serve me well enough most of the time. I tend not to fish when conditions demand strong-arm tactics, the thought of pulling hooks out of barbel, or any other fish, doesn't strike me as sporting angling. I would rather fish when and where I can catch fish causing them minimal damage.

Rigs

Hook lengths are critically important. The ideal material for all conditions hasn't arrived yet but Dacron, Merlin, Silkworm, Snakebite and other braids are very handy. 'Double strength' and Flourocarbon lines are very good when low visibility is an issue - float fishing, for instance. Make sure you moisten the knot before easing it tight. When knotting braid don't use strangulation knots like the blood knot, use the double grinner or Uni knot. Most braids come with a little leaflet with recommended knots - it's worth reading. See Steve Stayners book for more detail. For pinning your link to the bed or for delicate adjustments of float shotting try Kryston Heavy Metal Rig Putty - it really is very useful and, because it's re-usable, easily affordable. For rig set-ups, try some of the following ideas:

- Free-lined nylon line of 6lb bs straight through to an eyed barbless hook.

- As above with a shot or two pinched on, plus or minus a float.

- Free-lined with a hook shank wrapped with lead wire. This is buried in the bait and allows a leger-free but weighted rig for trundling over gravel runs. The amount of wire can be varied to suit the swim.

- A simple running leger with Arlesey bomb or drilled bullet, stopped a few inches from the hook.

- As above with a feeder in place of the lead. Trace length is varied until successful.
- As above but with a tangle-free feeder rig on a power gum loop or John Roberts low-resistance leger ring. A break-free lead link can be made from a loop of power gum.
- Tangles can be reduced by mounting the lead on a short length of rig tubing and a 'bolt rig' made by pushing the rig tube onto the end of the swivel.
- As above with a separate hook link of finer / softer nylon (flourocarbon, Berkeley XL, Drennan Double Strength) and smaller hook or with a braided or multi-strand link with swivel link to main line. Also with an in-line flattened Korda type lead.
- As above but with braid treated with anti-tangle gel or Rig-A-Mawtis or with Granite Juice to protect from abrasion on snags.
- As above but with a hair rig as part of the braided leader or pellet on rubber bait loop.
- As above but with 1lb bs line for hair rig and / or buoyancy built onto the hook with rig foam/cork to produce a neutrally-buoyant baited hook. Baits then waft around like free offerings. Deliberate extra buoyancy on the hook, eg with a small poly ball creates a pop-up rig.
- Hair-rigged boilie on braided link with 'stringer' of free offerings on a PVA (water soluble) string.
- Super glue or Kryston Bogey can be used to stick dry grains (eg hemp) or casters around a hook or around the hair or on a poly ball eg to create a maggot Medusa rig.
- Heavy Metal putty can be used in small balls on the trace running up to the hook to 'pin down' the trace to the bed. Back-leads can be used on the main line to flatten it down on the bed, reducing line bites and the spooking of shy barbel.
- Hook lengths can vary from 3inch pop-ups to ten feet long fine flourocarbon leaders.

In general, when experiencing difficulty in getting bites, lengthen and lighten your leader and reduce hook and bait size. Also, think about whether your bait can 'behave' in a reasonably lifelike manner. Be prepared to experiment and think about what is happening to the 'business end' of your tackle. See the excellent books by Roger Miller, Steve Stayner, John Baker and John Wilson for further discussions of lines, rigs and clever approaches to catching wary barbel.

Putting it all together - some fishy stories

> THERE'S ABOUT 7FT. OF WATER IN THE SWIM, SO I'LL SET THE FLOAT AT 8FT. THEN THE BAIT WILL DRAG BOTTOM

© MGN Ltd

The Dorset Stour

Throop

Throop on the lower Dorset Stour is a Mecca for barbel fishers. The fishery sees a lot of anglers and yet the stocks of barbel and chub remain prolific and of good quality. It is rare to catch a tatty fish - this just shows how resilient coarse fish stocks are. This autumn afternoon saw Dave (Anguilla) Wettner and myself wandering the banks in search of piscine interest. I photographed a six pound-plus chub for a very pleased Chub Study Group member fishing just below the boulder weir - he picked it up on feeder-fished maggots flavoured with Scopex. My white maggots were bog standard Avon Angling Centre's best and bunched about 8-up on a size 10. A grain of hemp held the maggots in place on the barbless hook. The rig was a simple straight through flat leger stopped above a braided 18 inch leader and cast mid-stream just where the channel narrows above the boulder weir. Here the current speed picks up creating a lie which barbel can easily hold in but which would make most other coarse fish species work hard. The touch-legered rig was set to move on the merest pull.

Around a 1/4 pint of maggots was fed into the swim over the course of half an hour and, I must confess, my concentration was wandering a little when I sensed a grating on the line. This went on for around 20 seconds and then stopped. I felt no pull at all. The grating then started again and I struck gently to find myself hooked firmly into a snag.....which then very slowly motored off upstream. Typically of a good barbel, that fish sat deep in the current with its fins fully extended, flying like a kite and giving me no line at all. This stalemate carried on for several minutes with my Davis Tackle Avon Special hooped fully around, then, grudgingly, the fish gave ground, ever so slowly upstream, towards me. Nothing spectacular happened, just very solid prolonged resistance with a couple of short downstream runs. Then, in the thin sunlight of the late afternoon a golden flank flashed deep down as the fish tired, rolled and came to the net - I couldn't resist landing and weighing this one as it was obviously a good fish....11lb 10oz, fin-perfect, like a newly-minted coin, hooked clean in the scissors. Superb. After the hard fight the fish needed supporting for a while head-upstream before it was ready to power away.

Points to note were the lack of a 'bite' - only touch legering would have caught this fish which was gingerly mouthing the bait and the fact that it fed during the day in reasonably bright sunlight. Dave caught a nice six pounder later in the evening from the run upstream of the bridge in the middle of the fishery - touch legered pink indispensable did the trick. 11lb 10oz is still my PB from the Stour although, this winter........

The Wye

John Bailey (see www.angling-travel.com) helped me to get to know the 'Red Lion' and associated syndicate water on the Wye around Bredwardine (see www.hay-on-wye.co.uk/redlion). I have been back several times since despite the 200 plus miles round-trip from deepest Dorset and have enjoyed every minute of it. The Wye is a fabulous river with tremendous potential for the footloose fisher willing to walk a mile or three and do some exploring. Mike Taylor the landlord of the Red Lion runs a happy ship. He has been lucky - the downturn in salmon stocks and interest in salmon fishing has been substituted by a new clientele of equally keen barbellers. On this occasion Ian (Ghandi) Watson, Nick (Matched Pair) Bubb and I had waded out onto a sandstone ledge adjacent to a long gulley which usually holds a barbel shoal. The water was around four to five feet deep at the deepest point and crystal clear. The wide river channel narrows into the mouth of the gully, speeding up the current over a clean gravel bed with sparse crowfoot growth. Perfect barbel habitat. By sitting well up the bank, amongst the trees, I could watch the reactions of the fish to baits - it was really fascinating. Ian and Nick were touch-legering corn or meat and feeding hemp regularly. The barbel were mopping up the free offerings and studiously avoiding the hook baits, several of the fish looked good doubles, one dark one which hung back in the shoal looked truly awesome....a third as big again as the fish which looked like doubles. Wow! There were around fifteen other smaller barbel which I guestimated at weighing four to ten pounds, mostly in the six to eight pound bracket.

From my high observation point I watched the shoal push upstream to raid the ground-baited area and then drop back before wheeling upstream again a few minutes later. The cycle was repeated time and again. Nick and Ian, fishing, at times, only 10 yards from the fish, and probably in view from time to time didn't seem to spook them at all. Because of the angle of the light they couldn't see the barbel from where they were fishing, at river level. The barbel were happily tucked into their favourite swim and felt safe, feeding well in sunlit conditions in late summer. What I was surprised to see was just how often those fish nudged and wafted the legered baits before rejecting them as suspect. Many dozens of times.....whilst Nick and Ian felt nothing at all through their carefully touch-legered tackle. How often does this sort if thing happen ? Quite a bit, I reckon.

I slid back down off the tree, through some nettles and across a slippery clay bank before landing next to my gear.....bugger ! The barbel fed on, quite happily. OK, fair enough, the aged B.James split cane Avocet was baited up with a big lump of Bacon Grill steeped in John Baker's Barbel Search 4 flavouring and a gentle upstream cast was allowed to trundle at current speed back across the gravel. No dice. This was repeated many times until a trembling, sawing sensation transmitted through the old cane turned into a full-blooded pull. Thus started a serious battle. That barbel hung in there for many minutes whilst the Maxima was tested to maximum by a Barbus maximus. I started to get a little anxious for my rod and so turned it over every so often to equalise the strain during the fight. I didn't want the old cane to end up looking like Bubb or Watson. Also, I decided to net the fish - both to have a look at whatever could pull that hard and to make sure that it wasn't too knackered to return safely.

Usually, I try to unhook fish in the water, holding them in the current before they swim away but I'm glad I checked this fish out as it was well tired when it finally graced Mr Bubb's net. A weigh in a sling gave 12lb 2oz, a PB for all rivers and, once again, in perfect nick. To top it all, Ian got a 12lb 4oz in the evening (also a PB) and we all ended up with four or five barbel - Mr Bubb narrowly missing a double. As far as Ian and I were concerned this was a just outcome reflecting skill and application but Nick didn't seem to agree totally. Fellow barbel fisher Tim Pryke looked on with amusement.

In true Red Lion tradition, Ian and I got our ties (awarded to double figure barbel catchers in the bar by a beaming Mike Taylor) whilst Bubb got the round in. He already had a tie.

Lessons from this trip were many:

- How often do we fish low-visibility swims unaware that barbel are inspecting and rejecting baits most of the time?

- Was it the trundling of baits which induced takes or the Search 4 flavouring or did the barbel just build up enough confidence to start taking hook baits confidently after prolonged feeding of the swim? I don't know.

- Were either of the 12 pounders the huge dark fish which I had seen earlier or were they a couple of the estimated doubles? If the latter - how big was the dark fish which we didn't catch!

A barbel called Harry

Again on the Wye, this time Bubb and Watson fishing on their own. The river high and coloured in autumn, forcing a strategy of fishing down the near side bank or pegging out a bait in the flow on the sort of leger you could tie the QE2 to in a force 9 gale. Bubb went for a nice undercut bank just downstream, rolling a leger in close under an alder and sitting back. In due course he hit a bite which turned into a mega-barbel which fought very hard for quite a while. The fish netted and unhooked, an excited Bubb carefully left the barbel in the net at the edge of the main flow to recover as he legged it down the bank to find Ian to witness the leviathan. Ian duly trotted back up with Nick to savour the magnificent fish, surely a PB amongst our group of chums, only to find that it had rolled the net over and escaped, unweighed and with no photo…..Harry Houdini.

Well, I guess we believe him; a disconsolate Bubb reckons that fish was 'much bigger' than our twelve pounders, but he would say that wouldn't he? He very much wants to catch it again and, knowing him, he probably will. Come to think of it, a barbel of those dimensions would, of course, be a Harriet.

Tim Pryke belongs to the barbel syndicate at the lower end of the Red Lion pub water - one of the beats is heavily wooded and steep-banked, difficult access to a shallow, fast, gravelly section of river. Tim was fishing during a very hot spell of weather and decided that barbel (if they had read the books) should be heading for fast, streamy, well-oxygenated water. The middle of the beat seemed ideal but how to fish it? Tim decided to hack a pathway down to the river through the thick vegetation, arriving breathless and perspiring on the bank some time later, having cunningly followed a side stream to ease his access. There on the shallows was a shoal of prime barbel lurking in the shallow, bubbly shaded waters. Tim arose very early the next morning, sneaking out of the pub and heading straight for his newly created swim. On arriving and wading in quietly he was treated to the sight of a shoal of big barbel just upstream - backs breaking out of the water, just waiting to be caught…..anticipation ran high. The tactic was free-lining a lobworm but with a small ball of stodgy groundbait to weight the tackle for casting. The bait would then be tweaked back downstream to the waiting barbel. Baldrick could not have come up with a more cunning plan.

The first cast was perfect…..the worm trickled back towards Tim and then there was a tingling on the line….a gentle strike connected and a half pound chub splashed its way down do a disappointed angler.

No problem though - still the barbel were happily cruising on the shallows and so another worm was lobbed upstream. Forty minutes later Tim was on his knees with frustration…..every cast produced a chublet whilst the barbel continued to roll, flash and swirl to their heart's content. About an hour later Tim was back in the Red Lion eating his breakfast in silence. Barbel fishing can be like that.

The Upper Bristol Avon

I grew up fishing the Bristol Avon around Bath on Bathampton Club waters (Claverton and Limpley Stoke) and have made occasional returns to fish it since. Stuart Morgan and friends have, in recent seasons, been banking barbel which we could only have dreamed of when I was a nipper. The habitat project on the river below Malmesbury (Chapter 4) gave me a good excuse to have another go, this time on the Somerford Club waters. Thanks are due to George Probert, the hard-working fishery manager, for permission to fish. Great Somerford weir pool is a well known spot - full of barbel from a pound up to double figures. I found these fish reasonably easy to catch on cheese paste and meaty pastes, clocking up some nice ones including occasional low doubles. My best catches were three or four fish in an evening and I was well pleased - somewhat more productive for me than a typical Hampshire Avon evening where one decent fish is a good night! What really opened my eyes at Great Somerford though was the power of pre-baiting to get barbel on the feed.

Two Game Conservancy colleagues, Dom and Reuben, had (unknown to me) been lacing the pool with fish meal pellets over the course of a few days when we all turned up for a couple of hours fishing before the long drive back to Fordingbridge. Quite by chance I chose to fish a John Roberts bait loop with a small trout pellet tight up to a barbless 12 hook on a braided leader. A light Arlesey bomb completed the simple rig. Having waded carefully out across the lip of the pool I sat on a rock and lobbed out the gear. No sooner had the tackle settled than the rod was nearly pulled out of my hand and a beautiful Avon barbel of around four pounds was brought to hand and slipped off the hook. Blinking in surprise I re-cast and did the same thing again, and again, and again. Every time the bomb settled it was off - bang, with another medium-sized bertie. I can't remember how many we caught between us but it was twenty plus and they were one after the other, all released in the water with minimal hassle. Great fun in good company.

The moral of the story for me was the change in behaviour of the fish to a modest pre-baiting period of just a few days. The smaller shoal barbel were hoovering up any fishy pellets they could get hold of. This is well worth transferring to your fishery - actively feeding barbel are so much easier to catch than ones which are a bit edgy. Another point to note though was that none of the bigger fish were caught by this mehod; whether this was down to the sheer numbers of smaller barbel after the bait or the wariness of the bigger fish, I don't know.

Finally, many of the fish had other hooks in their mouths and broken fine leaders dangling behind them. We removed all we could find. Why do some people use tackle which just isn't up to the job?

The Hampshire Avon

Ibsley

I'm lucky to live within a 15 minute drive of the Somerley Estate on the Hampshire Avon. We've been in Dorset for around ten years now and it's a nice neck of the woods for any fisherman to frequent. The Avon, the Stour, the lakes, Christchurch Harbour, the coastline - just great. Membership of Christchurch Angling Club (www.christchurchac.org) has to be the bargain of the year - contact Steve Richards on 01425 279701. As mentioned before, I haven't found the Avon easy to get to know but, over the years, my success rate has risen a fair bit. Even very good anglers (way above my competence) often find the Avon difficult so, if you too have struggled, don't give up. It's a fast-running, very clear, often shallow, very productive river with a patchy barbel stock - all in all, not easy. I've been lucky to get some tips from Chris (Golden Scale)Yates and other friendly locals who know the ropes. I believe that the key to Avon barbel success is location of fish plus getting them feeding confidently. Often, location has to be very accurate - miss the holding spot and you may as well be fishing without a hook. Ibsley, despite being close to the noisy Salisbury to Ringwood road, is a great section of river with a long angling history.

Many big fish still cruise around its waters. Dave Wettner was looking over Ibsley Bridge a while ago (as all true anglers do when they visit this spot) when he spotted a barbel well into double figures upside-down, hoovering the underneath of a crowfoot bed. What the fish was eating he couldn't make out but it was probably picking off snails or insect larvae. It's not unusual to see barbel, chub, salmon and even carp cruising around Ibsley Bridge. Some of the roach are well above the magic two pound mark.

On the downstream road side of the bridge is the bus stop swim - noisy from the traffic but deep and full of fish of many species. I sat there one evening with Garry (VAT) Lee and we were debating the best tactics. He opted for fishing light downstream under the bank with double maggot whilst I persevered further out with legered paste. The score ? Lee 1, Giles nil - a 10 pounder for Garry, much to his delight.

An interesting point from this capture was the probable benefit of light line and small hooks (3lb and size 16, I think) and the surprising amount of hammer that light gear will take if you are using a limber rod and are patient. The debate on just how strong your tackle needs to be to land barbel rages on. On balance, I like to fish with strong gear - braided hook lengths certainly help with presentation here but light line tactics can and do pay off. I suppose the nature of the swim is usually the deciding factor - no snags and plenty of room and light gear becomes a reasonable proposition. Also, of course, the size of the run-of-the-mill barbel is pretty important too.

John Bickerdyke had it sussed out back in 1888 (The book of the all-round angler) :

> *'I have only to add, or rather repeat, that our friend the barbel is very shy, and that fine fishing for him really pays. Unless the swim is in the midst of numerous tackle-destroyers, such as old piles, big stones, roots of trees, and the like, where large fish must be held - a process necessitating stout gut - use as fine tackle as you reasonably can, and if you ground bait with discretion, fish with patient carefulness, and rise early enough, you will, no doubt, catch many barbel, and enjoy grand sport.'*

Bickerdyke, all that time ago, also talked about the fact that big barbel like to live in safe places. Upstream of Ibsley Bridge Dave Wettner discovered the critical value of overhead cover. *I leave it to Dave to relate the story.....*

Mid-November 1999, wandering up the Avon with the low roar of Ibsley weir in the background it was a classic autumn barbel evening - mild, heavily overcast - almost steamy, with coloured water of rising temperature. The Avon is magnificent in autumn - far bank trees reflected golden, orange and ochre hues onto the smoothly flowing surface of the river. Little grebes diving and an iridescent kingfisher added to a perfect scene; the rumbling traffic on the A338 merged into the background.

I started fishing a smooth near bank glide overhung with the dying remnants of the summer's reed and rushes. Trundling a piece of luncheon meat along the edge I soon felt a sharp tug on the loop of line over my finger....missed it. Still, a bite first cast, success indeed. A few uneventful trundles later and a chunky chub put a bend in the old cane rod, boring underneath the bank before being netted. Lying in the damp grass, pewter and bronze tinted chain-mail and faintly pink fins - I don't care if they are inedible, I like chub!

Fishing my way back downstream an hour later I had only one more missed bite to add to my tally and the light was falling as I noticed a steady piece of water disappearing under a small bush which had recently fallen into the water. It was a testament to my watercraft skills that I hadn't noticed it on my way upstream. This looked like a chub's 'Ideal Home' ......maybe even a barbel's. A piece of flake tempted a chub out of his lair and, in true expert style, I changed bait to luncheon meat.....clearly the success was too much for me. The bait lay under the overhanging branches for just a few minutes before another bite, a solid resistance and the mental image of a golden barbel gracing my net was shattered by the appearance of monstrous writhing eel which thrashed across the surface before covering the net in slime.....why do chub and barbel cohabit with eels ?

Being extremely fond of eels, I rebaited with meat and flicked another cast under the bush, in the deepening gloom - the cane tip nodded and pulled down, this time the solid resistance enduring, not turning rapidly snake-shaped, as a powerful barbel moved slowly across the river. The chatter of the ratchet on the centre pin quietened and then sang again as the barbel headed for the horizon. Gently I coaxed the fish back across the river , however it had other ideas, exploring the far bank once again before tiring and rolling over the rim of the net....around ten pounds of pristine golden Avon barbel. Great!

Flushed with success and hungry for more eels I cast another lump of meat close to the bush, sat back and realised that it had become quite dark. The glow of a torch downstream showed that I wasn't the only one who thought it was a fishy evening. After about twenty minutes another solid pull on the line met with more heavy resistance, the reel again burst into life as another bronze monster thumped out into the river, moving slowly and sullenly unwilling to yield any line. Several minutes of thumps and short runs later it decided that maybe the cane did have the upper hand and slid over the net - a long, pale and whiskered shape reflecting the last of the evening light. On the bank the barbel grew in stature, expanding to fill the net and, not being a frequent catcher of large barbel, I decided to weigh it. A few ounces over eleven pounds.....for me, a monster !

The fellow barbel expert - because that is what I obviously now was ! - crept along the bank to photograph the fish, as it slipped back into the river I thought about packing up. But, as always, the 'last cast' was soon flying toward the fishy sanctuary and, within minutes another heavy barbel was wrenching line from the protesting centre pin. This time, however, after a busy ten minute tussle, the barbel won, slipping the hook and reminding me that, perhaps, I was being a little too greedy.

On the short walk back to Ibsley Bridge I reflected on the excellent mild conditions, the 'perfect' glide flowing under overhead cover - the barbel's 'Ideal home'. Next time I knocked on the door I was sure to get a thirteen pounder. Next time I walked the bank, however, the bush had gone.

Thanks Dave - what an evening, just think, most people were back home watching tv.

At the bottom of the track at Ibsley is Edwards Pool, a small pond full of lovely tench. Opposite this is a sharp loop on the Avon. Next to the Pool car park is a large slack which holds some superb barbel (and pike) in winter. Last year I tried a couple of times to catch these fish. I saw my biggest Avon barbel by far - well into double figures as it lazily rolled just out from my rod tip one evening. Could I catch it? No way. Time seems to stand still when the broad golden back of a big barbel rolls before your eyes........

If you wander along that bank you soon come to the corner swim where a side stream re-joins the main Avon. This swim is deep, gravel-bedded, with swirling crowfoot beds and overhanging willows on the far bank....barbel country. Location here is, once again, the key. During the day a bait cast right in under the far bank willows is the most likely to succeed whilst, around dusk, barbel come out all over the pool and gravel shallows just upstream. This pool has produced two double figure barbel for me and several smaller fish. In July this year, a double figure pike snaffled a red boilie as soon as it settled under a willow and then proceeded to give a very believable impression of a big barbel as it bored around in the current. I was sharing a swim with Dave. Mr Wettner was most amused when my face fell as the expected 'large barbel' slowly surfaced, materialising into an angry pike hooked square in the scissors. Pike - on boilies......whatever next?

Nick Bubb did a similar thing on the Kennet some seasons ago. We were 'barbelling' in a weir pool with lobworm when he hooked a good fish and confidently announced 'barbel'. I stood ready with the net as what was clearly a big fish led him a merry chase around the pool. At last it approached the lip of the net exposing a toothy grin followed by 20 pounds of pike, again, hooked neatly in the scissors. Two lads standing nearby looked agog at the awesome beast, one said - 'Blimey Mr - you'll be on the front page of the Angling Times with that one'.

On another trip Nick took an angling novice work colleague out for his first barbel trip, set him up with some feeder gear and left him to his own devices. After a while he noticed that the chap was only casting occasionally, with long gaps in between casts. A stroll up the bank to provide some helpful advice revealed a frustrated fisherman peering closely at his swim feeder and surrounded by a thin carpet of escaping maggots. When Nick asked him if all was well he replied:

'Yeah, really enjoying it, but it takes ages getting all these maggots into the feeder through all those tiny holes'.

Fordingbridge

Before going freelance as a fisheries and conservation consultant, for several years I ran the fisheries team at The Game Conservancy HQ in Burgate Manor on the banks of the Avon at Fordingbridge. As with so many anglers with fishing on their door step, I hardly ever fished it when I was there. I was too busy. The barbel were, however, sometimes easy to spot finning over the gravel glides amongst the crowfoot beds. Since then, however, I've got my priorities better sorted out and I'm quite keen on fishing one or two Avon stretches not far upstream. One of these is owned by the Sandy Balls Holiday Camp and it's a superb piece of water which I always reckoned looked good for a big barbel……..

The October 2nd 2001 Angling Times ran a story which is not believed by all locals but is worth an airing. 14 year-old Ryan Gibson was holidaying with his parents and was allowed to fish each evening on the river. Ryan is a good angler with some big carp under his belt but, until then, no barbel. He fished patiently each evening, baiting up with Activ-8 boilies and sitting quietly by the river for 10 nights on the trot with no success. His hair-rigged baits remained static. His perseverance was eventually rewarded, however, on the 11th night when his rod suddenly did an impression of an Exocet missile - Ryan was locked solid into a serious barbel which fought extremely strongly for 20 minutes on 10lb line. His carp fishing experience stood him in good stead and, not panicking, he played the fish out expertly. Dad, Steve eventually netted Ryan's first barbel which turned the scales at a whopping 16lb 4oz - an Avon record, not bad for a first fish! Ryan went on to catch a 14lb 5oz fish two nights later, again on boilies, just to show that his record fish was no fluke.

What is the moral of this story?

- If at first you don't succeed, keep on keeping on.
- Sit quietly and bait up a swim with something interesting but unusual bait-wise.
- Maintain confidence in your approach and keep feeding your swim.
- Don't think you have to have expensive gear - Ryan's barbel were caught on a quiver tip rod bought for £15 at a car boot sale a few weeks earlier.

I can't help smiling when I think of the time and expense which many a well known barbel specimen hunter has gone to on the Avon trying to track down a river record fish. I'll bet none of them used a 15 quid car boot sale rod!

I leave Christchurch AC Chairman Pete Reading the last words on Avon barbelling - he knows much more about it than I do:

In praise of barbel fishing

There has never been a more exciting time to be a barbel fisherman, with the species being more widespread and accessible to anglers than ever before, and with growth rates rising rapidly in recent years, for whatever reason. Anglers seeking good barbel fishing now no longer need to travel great distances to find their fish, and the records that stood for decades at a little over fourteen pounds are now surpassed more than once each season. More anglers than ever are becoming interested in barbel, and many will find themselves falling under the spell of the barbel, fishing for the species in exclusion of all others for some time, or maybe even for a lifetime as has happened to some.

The attraction of the barbel is not difficult to explain. They are an elegant yet powerful species, hard biting and hard fighting, and unlike the carp they can still be found in a wild state; there are still stretches of river where unknown and uncaught barbel can be imagined and sought out. The hard-fished stretches will, of course, hold fish with names that can be targeted clinically by anglers perhaps themselves seeking a name, but the fact that the barbel is a river fish by nature means that he is still free to roam and take up residence in areas where thought and watercraft, rather than an anglers mere presence and persistence, can lead to his capture. This is the real attraction of the barbel to me nowadays, the chance to explore and find new shoals or hopefully big fish that may not have been hooked much before, although restriction in available fishing time does not permit the purposeful hunting of new fish to take up too much of it!

There is also a significant challenge in catching fish that are well fished for, and most barbel in the more popular rivers are likely to be aware of us and our attempts to catch them. There is nothing wrong with a visit to a well known swim or fishery to try and get a few fish under your belt after a few sessions of fruitless searching for the elusive unknown barbel. Indeed, the Royalty barbel is likely to be much more difficult to catch than an unsuspecting fish from a little fished stretch of the river. Fishing the clear Southern rivers like the Hampshire Avon and Dorset Stour means that in summer, at least, the fish can be spotted and observed a lot of the time, another reason why we like fishing for them so much. Watching fish taking, or more often, not taking your bait is a thrill particular to the barbel or chub angler, and sometimes seeing the peculiar mix of predictable and inexplicable behaviour of barbel can be more pleasurable than the catching of them!

The summer barbel is usually eager to feed, and it is very gratifying to see a shoal of fish that you may have found apparently resting and inactive, rooting around in the gravel to get your introduced feed down their necks as soon as possible. Barbel respond very positively to bait most of the time, and I have seen them rip up weed beds, move stones the size of a house brick and scour gravel to shining yellow in their efforts to get to food.

In thick weed it is possible to locate them by looking out for clouds of disturbed mud and silt as they forage about for loose-fed hemp or other particles bait-dropped into likely areas. The vigour with which they feed at times can make them seem easy to catch, and indeed they are when it suits them.

At other times, they can be incredibly spooky, and I have emptied a swim of barbel merely by flicking in two or three grains of sweetcorn. There are swims on the Great Ouse where the sight of a bait-dropper will put the fish out of the swim and in hiding for hours, or an inopportune, poorly timed cast will send a previously greedily feeding fish into a frightened sulk for the whole of the day. It is not only pressured fish that can be unresponsive and awkward customers, the well fed and relaxed barbel will often ignore new food items with total disdain, and it is not so long ago that I fed hemp into the Hampshire Avon for the first time, and it was probably the first time that those barbel had seen it. They ignored it completely, going so far as to have a bit of a grub round in a nearby weedbed for some caddis or snails or some other natural item. It took a lot of heavy baiting before they took to hemp, but once they switched on they became absolute suckers.

Nowadays we hear of barbel that are really quite scared of hemp, due to intense fishing pressure, and the hard fished stretches of the Bristol Avon, for example, now respond better to trout pellet or other particles as attractors. Barbel like to eat a wide range of food items, and this means that there are aficionados of as wide a range of baits and techniques to capture them. They are clearly quite adept at eating tiny particles of food, and are well adapted to separating bits of food from the substrate on which they are feeding. It is common to see them blowing sand or small gravel out of their mouths and gills, and there must be some complex sorting process going on inside that cavernous mouth; I have always imagined it to be based on the density of the particles, in effect they use the same principle as panning for gold, perhaps. Barbel can spot and take small individual food items, though, and I have seen them rise to midwater from the bottom of the river to take a single maggot.

On the other hand, they will eat big baits too, and my most memorable example was of a fish of about eight pounds making off with a quarter chicken discarded by a dissatisfied diner from a riverside pub at Longham on the Dorset Stour. I was in fact watching the chub that were mopping up the chips from the same meal when the barbel hove into view and grabbed the remainder of the basket meal. You can fish with the particle approach, with maggot, caster, hemp or pellet, or rove with big lumps of meat or boilies between pre-baited swims; you can trundle or trot, or sit behind a couple of rods with baits nailed to the bottom. The beauty of barbel and barbel fishing is that you can choose from a variety of approaches, baits and methods that suit your river, your preferences and your lifestyle.

Thanks Pete, well said.

The Great Ouse

I worked for a while at the Great Linford Wildfowl Centre where we carried out ecological research on gravel pit fish and wildfowl populations. In those days the ever-friendly Len Gurd ran the fishing there and, with typical generosity, he let us fish from time to time. I wasn't really into barbel fishing in those days, preferring instead to catch carp and tench from the lakes but what I did enjoy was a lunchtime or early evening wander to go chub and barbel spotting. Once again, the big lesson to learn was the love that adult barbel and chub have for dense overhead cover. You could walk for half a mile scanning the gravel bed of the Ouse for big fish in open water and draw a blank. Then, under an alder or goat willow a pod of several barbel and chub would be tucked right in under the tree roots keeping well out of the way. Under cover of darkness they ventured out to roam the gravel shallows. Little did I realise that, 15 or so years later, the Ouse a little way downstream would be turning up a string of record-breaking barbel.

Whilst working at Linford we lived in Buckingham where I often canoed upstream of the town on the Ouse in the summer evenings - chub spotting. It's amazing how close you can get to shy big chub in a canoe - they just don't seem to associate them with danger. The upper Ouse is well known as a big chub river - Dick Walker had a fishing hut at Thornborough for a number of years. Several things became apparent to me as I got to know a two to three mile stretch which runs through farmland and is hardly fished. The medium-sized chub (two to three pounders) shoal up in pools, the bigger fish (four to five pounders) live in deep cover where you can still see them if you are careful but the biggest chub (six pounds plus) you virtually never see. These fish are so shy and careful that they live in total cover, venturing out at night to feed. How do I know they were there I hear you ask? The answer is rather sad.

Having canoed and fished the river for several years, I thought I knew it pretty well. Then, one summer day, a farmer way upstream washed out a spray tank on a ford in the river. A choking cloud of pesticide drifted downstream, killing most big fish in its path (many smaller ones survived). Out from under bridges and undercut banks appeared a few massive wild brown trout and chub - six and seven pounders which nobody knew were there. And there they died, victims of one small accidental pollution which could so easily have been avoided. Lessons learnt for me were : Don't assume that just because you haven't seen any leviathans they aren't there and, do everything you can to explain the dangers of water pollution to farmers and other riparian owners. One mistake, made out of ignorance, and a generation of specimen fish can be wiped out. Very sad but, I'm afraid, not that uncommon.

Remember the Environment Agency Freephone emergency line : 0800 807060 - give them a call if you see fish in distress, they may be able to avert disaster on your fishery.

What individual barbel tell us

On all well-fished waters the anglers in the know get to recognise some of the bigger fish - usually those with a distinctive feature such as fin or scale damage or the presence of skin growths or pigments. Some of these fish have been caught many times and some over a long run of years. Key lessons for us as anglers and for those who are anti-angling to note include :

- Barbel can live for twenty or, perhaps exceptionally, 30-plus years. These big old fish gain and lose condition, depending on local circumstances and may hardly grow in length for many a long year.

- The same barbel can be caught many times over several years and continue to grow and remain in good condition. Catch-and-release barbel fishing is sustainable and, with due care, poses no threat to barbel stocks. It is unlikely that capture traumatises the fish too badly as they tend, generally, to thrive even on busy fisheries. Good handling is, however, important.

- In late winter big (female) barbel can weigh a pound and a half or more than they do in summer - this is due to loss of condition and eggs during the spring spawning, recovery in summer and rich autumn/winter feeding and the maturing of a new batch of eggs.

- Anglers baits help barbel to maintain growth and condition in many, or, perhaps, most rivers.

- Barbel, big and small are protected by anglers who care for their fisheries. Wildlife which also lives on those fisheries shares in this benefit.

Care of barbel

Barbel are delicate, long-lived fish which, like any other animal, demand respect. It is a privilege to catch them and, if we look after them, we may be lucky enough to catch them again when they are bigger. If you manage a barbel fishery, try to spread the angling effort out, rather than putting intense pressure on a few hotspots or on a couple of specimen fish. There are many ways of achieving this. The following points are worth noting :

- Manage the fishery to have a wealth of cover and holding spots - spread out the fish.
- Keep angling pressure within reasonable bounds - swims with no grass left on the bank are not a good sign that all is well.
- If a specimen barbel is getting caught often and is losing condition, then close the swim for a while to let it recover. Many barbel seem unwilling to forsake their favourite lie, despite intense angling pressure. Give them a break!
- Use adequate tackle and play the fish firmly so as not to tire it out too much. If you can, slip the hook out without taking the fish out of water - gills don't work very well in air and fish are more scared when on dry land.
- If releasing fish in the water, make sure they are not too tired to swim away strongly - hold them head-upstream for a while until they have 'caught their breath'.
- Using barbless hooks makes releasing fish much easier - very few fall off, despite the lack of a barb. A barb squeezed flat is a good half-way house.

Believe Andy Orme (Barbel Mania) :

' To barb or not to barb? I do not, but I buy barbed hooks and squeeze the barbs down to leave a small bump........The theoretical disadvantage is that they may fall out of a hooked fish but this has never happened to me in many years of barbel fishing.'

I use barbless hooks straight from the packet and have never had a barbel fall off the end - my chums would have you believe that this is because I catch so few anyway..... with friends like those....

- If landing fish, use a knotless net, lay the fish on a wet plastic sheet / unhooking mat and keep it out of the water for a minimum amount of time.

- Take special care not to damage the eyes which are vulnerable, also, try not to split fins or dislodge scales, both will re-grow but leave the fish open to infection until they heal over.

- Support the fish's head into the current until it is ready to swim away strongly. Some anglers use rigid staked-out tubes to allow their barbel to recover before release….whatever keeps the fish in best shape is the right answer.

Remember, it takes at least ten years for barbel to become whoppers - these fish are worth looking after.

I wish you tight lines in your hunt for Bertie.

© Bernard Venables

CHAPTER
6
Recommended reading

© Clare Yates

The Barbel Fisher - official magazine of the Barbel Society.

John Bailey (1994) **The Fishing Detective**. Collins Willow.

John Baker **Carp & Barbel Baits** - leaflet. High Trees, 4 Dark Lane, Wargrave, Reading, Berks.

John Baker (2001) **Modern barbel baits and tactics**. Address above or phone 01189 404837.

Baras,E (1993) **Thermal related variations of seasonal and daily spawning periodicity in** *Barbus barbus*. Journal of Fish Biology (1993) 46, 915-917

Baras, E, Lambert, H, & Phillipart, J-C (1994) **A comprehensive assessment of the failure of barbel (*Barbus barbus*) spawning migrations through a fish pass in the canalised River Meuse (Belgium)**. Aquat. Living Resour. &, 181-189.

Baras, E (1996) **Importance of gravel bars as spawning grounds and nurseries for European running water cyprinids**. Proceedings of 2nd IAHR Symposium on Habitat hydraulics, Ecohydraulics 2000, Quebec, Canada.

John Bickerdyke (1888) **The book of the all-round angler.** L. Upcott Gill, 170, Strand London.

Bischoff, A & Scholten, M. (1996) **Diurnal distribution patterns of 0+ barbel** *Barbus barbus* **in different types of habitats in the River Seig, Germany.** Folia Zoologica 45 (Supplement 1) pages 13-20.

Archie Braddock (1992) **Fantastic Feeder Fishing.** Pisces Press.

Patrick Chalmers (1932) **At the tail of the weir.** Philip Alan.

Gordon Copp & Tony Bennetts **Short-term effects of removing riparian and instream cover on barbel (*Barbus barbus*) and other fish populations in a stretch of English chalk stream.** Folia Zoologica 45(3): 283-288.

Cowx, I.G., Wheatley,G.A. & Mosely, A.S. (1986) **Long-term effects of land drainage works on fish stocks in the upper reaches of a lowland river.** Journal of Environmental Management (1986) 22, 147-156.

Ian Cowx & Robin Welcomme (eds) **Rehabilitation of rivers for fish.** Fishing News Books.

John Gierach (1986) **Trout Bum.** Pruett Publishing Co. Boulder, Colorado, USA.

Fred Crouch (1986) **Understanding Barbel.** Pelham Books Ltd.

Hugh Falkus & Fred Buller (1975) **Freshwater Fishing.** MacDonald & Janes.

David Carl Forbes (1967) **Catch a Big Fish.** Newnes.

John Goddard's **Waterside Guide** (1988). Unwin Hyman.

Nick Giles (1994) **Freshwater Fish of the British Isles.** Swan Hill Press.

Nick Giles & David Summers (1996) **Helping fish in lowland streams.** Game Conservancy Trust, Fordingbridge, Hants, SP6 1EF.

Nick Giles (1998) **Freshwater Fisheries and Wildlife Conservation : A good practice guide.** Environment Agency.

Frank Guttfield (1978) **The Big Fish Scene.** Ernest Benn.

R.S.Hancock, J.W.Jones & R.Shaw (1976) A preliminary report on the spawning behaviour and nature of sexual selection in the barbel, *Barbus barbus*. Journal of Fish Biology 9, 21-28.

Martin Hooper (1993) **Specimen Angling by Design.** Crowood Press.

William Howes (1960) **The Quest for Barbel.** Thorsons.

P.C.Hunt & J.W.Jones (1974) A population study of *Barbus barbus* in the River Severn, England I. Densities. Journal of Fish Biology 6, 255-267.

P.C.Hunt & J.W.Jones (1974) A population study of *Barbus barbus* in the River Severn, England II. Movements. Journal of Fish Biology 6, 269-278.

P.C.Hunt & J.W.Jones (1975) A population study of *Barbus barbus* in the River Severn, England III. Growth. Journal of Fish Biology 7, 361-376.

Martyn Lucas & Emma Batley (1996) Seasonal movements and behaviour of adult barbel, *Barbus barbus*, a riverine cyprinid fish : implications for river management. Journal of Applied Ecology 1996, Volume 33, pages 1345-1358.

Martyn Lucas & Emma Batley (1997) Effects of a flow-gauging weir on the migratory behaviour of adult barbel, a riverine cyprinid. Journal of Fish Biology 1997, Volume 50, pages 382-396.

Roger Miller (1996) **The Complete Barbel Angler.** The Crowood Press.

Tony Miles & Trefor West (1991) **Quest for barbel.** & 2nd Edition, The Crowood Press.

Andy Orme (1990) **Barbel Mania.** The Crowood Press.

Andy Orme (1994) **Roving for Barbel.** SEER RODS Ltd.

Philippart, J.C. & E. Baras (1996) **Comparison of tagging and tracking studies to estimate mobility patterns and home range in *Barbus barbus*.** Underwater Biotelemetry - Proceedings of the First conference and workshop on fish telemetry in Europe. University of Liege, Belgium, December 1996.

Mark, W. Pilcher & Gordon Copp (1997) **Winter distribution and habitat use by fish in a regulated lowland river system of south-east England.** Fisheries Management and Ecology (1997), 4, 199-215.

Pete Rogers (1994) **Red Letter Days.** Crowood.

Steve Stayner (2001) **The ultimate big barbel experience.** Harrison Advanced Rods, 201, Summers Road, Brunswick Business Park, Liverpool, L3 4BL

S.Swales & K.O'Hara (1983) **A short-term study of the effects of a habitat improvement programme on the distribution and abundance of fish stocks in a small lowland river in Shropshire.** Fisheries Management 14, No.3, 135-144.

C.R.Tyler & S.Everett (1993) **Incidences of gross morphological disorders in barbel (*Barbus barbus*) in three rivers in southern England.** Journal of Fish Biology (1993) 43, 739-748.

Bernard Venables (1949) **Mr Crabtree goes Fishing.** Daily Mirror.

Waterlog - Magazine for the absolute angler.

Richard Walker (1964) **No need to lie.** EMAP.

Richard Walker (1981) **Catching fish knowing their feeding habits.** David & Charles.

Watkins, M.S., Doherty, S. & Copp, G.H. (1997) **Microhabitat use by 0+ and older fishes in a small English chalk stream.** J. Fish Biology, 50, 1010-1024.

Peter Wheat (1967) **The Fighting Barbel.** Ernest Benn Ltd.

Peter Wheat (1967) **Fishing as we find it.** Frederick Warne & Co Ltd.

Alwynne Wheeler & David Jordan (1990) **The status of the Barbel,**

Barbus barbus L.(Teleostei, Cyprinidae), in the United Kingdom. Journal of Fish Biology.

John Wilson (1992) **Catch Barbel.** Angling Times / Boxtree Ltd.

John Wilson (1997) **John Wilson's coarse fishing method manual.** Boxtree.

Chris Yates (1990) **The Deepening Pool.** Unwin Hyman Ltd.

Chris Yates, Bob James, Hugh Miles (1993) **A Passion for Angling.** Merlin Unwin/BBC.

Chris Yates (1998) **The River Prince.** Medlar Press Ltd.

© Clare Yates

This book is available from:

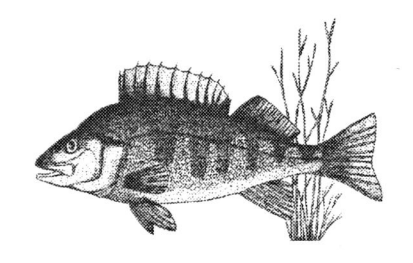

Perca Press, 50 Lake Road, Verwood, Dorset, BH31 6BX.

Tel 01202 824245 · Fax 01202 828056 · e-mail nickgiles@cix.co.uk

£ 15.50 inc. p&p, please make cheques payable to N. Giles.

Perca Press is an imprint of:

Dr Nick Giles & Associates,

50 Lake Road,
Verwood,
Dorset,
BH31 6BX.

Telephone 01202 824245
Fax   01202 828056
email nickgiles@cix.co.uk

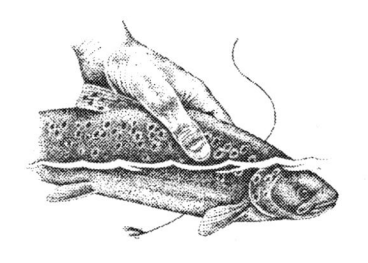

Consultants:
Freshwater Fisheries, Conservation & Wetland Ecology